MW01003148

Modern

Japanese

Tanka

An Anthology

Edited and Translated by

MAKOTO UEDA

Columbia

University

Press

New York

Columbia University Press

New York   Chichester, West Sussex

Copyright © 1996 by Columbia University Press

English translation rights arranged through
Makoto Ueda/Japan Foreign-Rights Centre.

The publisher wishes to thank Mr. Yoshiharu Fukuhara,
president and CEO *of Shisheido Co. Ltd., a member*
of the Association of 100 Japanese Books, for his contribution
toward the cost of publishing this translation.

Library of Congress Cataloging-in-Publication Data

Modern Japanese tanka : an anthology / compiled, translated, and with
an introduction by Makoto Ueda.
p.   cm. — (Modern Asian literature series)
Includes bibliographical references.
ISBN 0-231-10432-4 (alk. paper). — ISBN 0-231-10433-2 (alk.
paper)
1. Waka — Translations into English.   2. Japanese poetry — 1868 —
Translations into English.   3. Waka — History and criticism.
4. Japanese poetry — 1868–   — History and criticism   I. Ueda,
Makoto, 1931–   . II. Series.
PL782.E3M66   1996
895.6′1008 — dc20   95-40016
                                                     CIP

Casebound editions of Columbia University Press books are
printed on permanent and durable acid-free paper.

Printed in the United States of America

c 10 9 8 7 6 5 4 3 2 1
p 10 9 8 7 6 5 4 3 2

Contents

Preface

This is a collection of four hundred *tanka* written by twenty poets of modern Japan. Like haiku, tanka is an unrhymed Japanese verse form with a fixed syllabic pattern, but it is longer than haiku and has units of five, seven, five, seven, and seven syllables, arranged in that order. While haiku depends largely on the evocative power of images for its poetic effect, tanka tends to be more lyrical and expresses emotion in a wider variety of ways, not excluding imagist techniques. It is less restrictive than haiku, too, in that it requires neither a season word nor a *kireji* (cutting word). Usually it is printed in one continuous line, although it is often written in multiline form when it is presented as a work of calligraphy. Also, some radical poets in modern times have used such techniques as line changes and indentations to enhance certain poetic effects.

On rare occasions, the term *waka* is used interchangeably with tanka. However, the standard practice in today's Japan is to reserve the former term for the thirty-one-syllable poems written prior to the tanka reform that started in the late nineteenth century. In other words, tanka is modern and modernized waka. The historical development of waka is outlined in the introduction.

In selecting twenty modern poets, I have tried to sample all the major styles in which tanka has been written over the last one hundred years. Quite likely, however, my own taste has affected the choice. Those who find their favorite poets missing from this collection are encouraged to compile their own anthologies. There have been too few tanka available in English translation, and I would be delighted if this book could serve as a stimulus in this regard.

Japanese names, except my own, appear in the Japanese order, the surname preceding the given name or the gō, a name used in literary and artistic activities. Each author's poems are arranged roughly in chronological order. I say "roughly," because not all the poems have been datable. Original poems in romanized Japanese are appended at the bottom of each page. A solidus indicates a line change, and an extra space after a solidus signifies an indentation.

I am indebted to a number of individuals and organizations in the compilation of this anthology. My special thanks are due to Mr. Fukuhara Yoshiharu, president of Shiseido, for his generous contribution made through the good offices of the Association for 100 Japanese Books. A travel grant from the School of Humanities and Sciences at Stanford University enabled me to make a research trip to Japan in the summer of 1993. The East Asian Collection at the Hoover Institution provided me with many books of poetry and criticism I needed. The Japan Foreign-Rights Centre and its Managing Director, Miss Akiko Kurita, were most efficient in securing copyright permissions for me. I am also deeply grateful to Mr. J. M. B. Edwards, who carefully went over the entire manuscript and offered countless valuable suggestions, and to two anonymous readers for Columbia University Press, whose constructive critique was most helpful to me in revising the manuscript to its present form. Last but not least, I wish to thank Japanese scholars whose published commentaries on individual tanka solved many problems I had in understanding the text.

M. U.

Introduction

Some people have been fighting to have licensed prostitution abolished. Others are campaigning to outlaw the sale of liquor. How is it, then, that no one has tried to start a movement to ban the waka of our time? Strong as my words may sound, I am not overstating the case. Indulgence in drinking or in carnal pleasure harms the body in a way obvious to all. Indulgence in a certain type of poetry corrupts the spirit so unobtrusively that it goes unnoticed. Whereas the former kind of indulgence may lead to the loss of one's life, the latter kind may bring the entire nation to the brink of collapse.

Such were the opening words of a short article published in a prominent Tokyo newspaper on May 11, 1894. The article, part of a longer essay entitled "Bōkoku no on" (Poetry that Imperils the Nation), was from the pen of a staff writer who was just twenty-one years old. The young man, known as Yosano Tekkan (1873–1935), had long been irritated at the current state of the thirty-one-syllable verse known as *waka* and felt the time had come for him to take a stand. He did just that in this essay, backing up his argument by citing a number of waka written by well-known poets of the time and showing how mediocre these works appeared on close examination.

As Tekkan saw it, the most serious failing of contemporary waka poets was their lack of originality. "They imitate earlier poets in everything they do," he charged.

"They compete with each other merely by their skill in imitation." To make the situation worse, most waka poets took their models from undistinguished works of earlier times. The result was lifeless, uninspiring poetry that expressed trite emotions in stereotyped diction. From today's point of view, Tekkan's argument is so obviously justified that little need be added to it. Perhaps he related poetry a little too directly to the fate of the nation, but it should be remembered that nationalistic sentiments were unusually strong at the time, that Japan was on the brink of war with China, and that all activities were expected to contribute to the country's cause.

Tekkan was not the only poet who had become concerned with the sad state of waka. A number of other young poets shared the same concern, although none dared to verbalize it in such vehement words. In time they came to form several groups, each pushing for the reform of waka in a different way. Although the groups never united, there was a shared feeling that the new type of waka was so markedly different from the traditional one that a new name was needed for it. The name they tacitly agreed on was *tanka*. As the reform movements steadily gained in power and influence, the new name also gained public sanction. By 1910, tanka had established itself as a viable genre of modern Japanese literature.

Before the Reform

The origin of waka is as old as Japanese history itself. According to a myth recorded in Japan's oldest book, *Kojiki* (The Record of Ancient Matters), a brother of the sun goddess intoned the following thirty-one syllables when he had a house built for his bride:

here, where eight clouds rise   *yakumo tatsu*
in the land of Izumo   *Izumo yaegaki*

I will house my beloved	*tsumagomi ni*
inside an eightfold fence	*yaegaki tsukuru*
inside an eightfold fence	*sono yaegaki wo*

Today's scholars believe that the poem was really a communal song celebrating the building of a house for newlyweds. Apparently the author of the book took the song out of its social context and wove it into the texture of a myth. Because *Kojiki* is known to have been completed in 712 A.D., it can be surmised that the prototype of the thirty-one-syllable verse existed already in the oral literature of the seventh century or earlier. Poems in the same form are scattered throughout documents surviving from the early eighth century, along with pieces showing other syllabic patterns.

Predilection for the 5-7-5-7-7 form became more pronounced in the earliest anthology of Japanese verse, *Man'yōshū* (The Collection of Ten Thousand Leaves), which was compiled in the middle of the eighth century. Of some 4,500 poems that make up the collection, over 4,200 are written in the waka form. It is not clear why this particular form grew so popular, although its shortness may be attributed to the native Japanese prosody, which depended heavily on the repetition of five- and seven-syllable units. Because Japanese syllables are all evenly stressed, a long poem consisting of many such units could easily fall into monotony. Despite the prosodic uniformity, topics and sentiments presented in these poems show great variety, as the authors range from emperors and princes to frontier guards, fishermen, and even beggars. These poets expressed themselves in a powerful language, deriving power from their heartfelt emotion, simple vocabulary, and artless style. The results were poignant lyrics presenting a wide range of emotional responses to events, scenes, and aspects of the human condition. The finest poems in *Man'yōshū* provide precisely the kind of poetic norms emulated by later poets with a nostalgia for primitive culture.

During the next several centuries waka gradually evolved into court poetry, as the nation's literary and cultural activities came to be centralized in the imperial court. The thirty-one-syllable form became so prevailing that all the other forms were marginalized or driven to extinction. Working within that short form, poets tried to sharpen their poetic sensibilities, refine their language and metaphor, and achieve courtly types of beauty favoring elegance, harmony, and subtle humor. While they had little or no concept of lineation, they knew how to make effective use of the caesura that occurred at the end of each five- or seven-syllable unit. Treating prose as something complementary to verse, they freely prefaced their poems with headnotes of varying lengths, thereby creating proper contexts and compensating for the brevity of the waka. Although they scrupulously avoided using sinified words, they enriched their subject matter, imagery and technique by learning from the Chinese poetry of the Six Dynasties and T'ang periods. They also began developing the art of association and progression for structuring a sequence of waka.

The results of all these efforts are clearly manifest in the next important anthology of verse, *Kokinshū* (The Collection of Ancient and Modern Poems), which was presented to the imperial court in 905. Of the 1,100 poems that constituted the collection, all but nine were written in thirty-one syllables. Compared with *Man'-yōshū*, these poems are markedly more homogeneous in theme, sentiment, and diction, because the large majority of the authors had aristocratic family and educational backgrounds. Waka had become the poetry for court nobles, and in that sense its world had shrunk. On the other hand, that fact enabled poets, who now shared a narrower range of poetic ideals, to cultivate a rhetoric of omission and convey considerably more than what they expressly stated in their poems. It also encouraged them to display ingenuity in treating subjects, dexterity in articulating emotion, and urbane wit in addressing the reader. Poetry represented the crowning glory of human civilization, and waka, as its dominant form, was to show the ultimate expression of art and artifice. *Kokinshū*, the first anthology of verse compiled by an official imperial order, let the nation know that waka was the highest of all the arts.

Twenty more anthologies of Japanese poetry, of which an overwhelming majority was written in thirty-one syllables, were compiled under imperial auspices during the five hundred fifty years that followed. For their own pleasure, a number of prominent poets put together private waka collections, too. Although in the twelfth century court aristocrats were replaced by warrior cliques in political power, waka's high social esteem remained unchanged because an ideal samurai was expected to be skilled not only in military arts but also as a poet. Waka continued to be exchanged between friends, lovers, and even enemies who met on the battlefield. The thirty-one-syllable poem also provided aesthetic ideals and common sources of reference for other genres of literature, such as prose narrative, drama, and criticism.

Of the later poetry collections, the most highly admired was the eighth imperial anthology, *Shin kokinshū* (The New Collection of Ancient and Modern Poems), compiled in 1205 and comprising 1,978 poems written exclusively in the waka form. Restricted not only by the syllable count but by the centuries-long tradition of court poetry, waka poets had by this time been driven to explore the farthest boundaries of the verse form. The finest of the *Shin kokinshū* poets were marvelously successful in their explorations. Still emulating the traditional ideals, they were able to reinvigorate the thirty-one-syllable form through innovative use of such devices as classical allusion, wordplay, and symbolism. Through classical al-

lusion, they could create novel comparisons or contrasts
that would expand the meaning of their poems. Through
wordplay, they could bring together two disparate ideas
or images and thereby evoke unusual associations.
Through the use of symbols that vaguely referred to
things remote and unearthly, they could transport the
reader's imagination. Poetic techniques such as these had
been used in earlier poetry, but never to this extent or
with such dramatic effect. Because they sought novelty
above all else, the waka poets of this period were forced
to pursue every available poetic device to its limit.

Not surprisingly, the supreme artistry of the *Shin
kokinshū* poetry was never to be matched in the centuries
that followed. With no new areas left to explore within
the thirty-one-syllable form, many talented poets of later
times chose to try their hands in other genres. Thus in
the fourteenth and fifteenth centuries the verse form that
dominated the poetic scene was not waka but *renga*, a
sequence of one hundred stanzas composed by a team of
poets working under certain prescribed rules. The new
verse still used the subject matter of classical court po-
etry, but its greater length and multiple authorship en-
abled it to do a number of things the waka form could
not do. Then in the sixteenth century a genre of poetry
known as *haikai* branched off from renga and cultivated
thematic areas left unexplored in court poetry. Because
of its broadened subject matter, the new genre attracted
the interest of the plebeian class and became the most
popular form of verse in the seventeenth and eighteenth
centuries. Waka fell into a steady decline. There were a
small number of exceptions, most notably the works of
some eighteenth-century classicists who wrote in a style
reminiscent of *Man'yōshū*. Yet the vast majority of poems
composed by reputed waka masters were little more than
lifeless imitations of what had been written before—ex-
actly as Tekkan was to point out.

The outlook for waka became even less favorable after

Western literature began to reach Japan in the late nine-
teenth century. It took no time for Japanese readers to
become fascinated by European poetry, which was first
introduced in the 1880s through translations. The Japa-
nese were impressed, above all, by its rich intellectual
content, serious moral implications, uninhibited emo-
tional expression, and great freedom of form. In compari-
son, the Japanese poetry they knew seemed restrictive,
superficial, and antiquated. Some pessimists came to pre-
dict that traditional verse forms would not survive. They
were partially right, because renga became virtually ex-
tinct in the early twentieth century. Waka, bound by all
kinds of conventional rules, seemed about to follow suit
unless drastic measures were taken to modernize it. For-
tunately, there were Tekkan and other young poets who
firmly believed in the viability of waka, and they set about
reforming it so that it would respond to the emotional
needs of those living in the modern era. They succeeded,
and in time classical waka was reborn as modern tanka.

The Modern Romantics

Different groups of poets went different ways in their
effort to modernize the thirty-one-syllable form. The
most radical among them was the group led by Yosano
Tekkan, who tried to inject new life into the genre by
writing what he called *jiga no shi* or "poetry of the self."
As has been noted, Tekkan considered lack of originality
the greatest flaw of contemporary waka. Naturally, then,
his tanka of the future had to have plenty of originality,
which he thought would be afforded by the poet's indi-
viduality. Reared in a feudalistic society that demanded
sacrifice of the self, he conceived the new age to be more
humanistic and amenable toward assertion of individual-
ity, and the new type of poetry he envisioned was to
reflect that. When he published his first book of poetry
in 1896, he wrote in his preface: "My poetry, varied as it

is in style, has neither a teacher it follows nor a model it imitates. My poem is *my* poem." Four years later Tekkan and his group founded a new poetry magazine called *Myōjō* (The Morning Star) to promote the kind of poems they advocated. The magazine immediately became popular among young poets who had been unhappy with their environment. The newly introduced Western poetry, which seemed to allow self-expression far more freely than traditional Japanese verse, also helped to promote their cause. In particular the work of English romantic poets, such as Wordsworth, Shelley, and Byron inspired them with its strong assertion of the ego, passionate pursuit of the ideal, and defiant attitude toward existing social and moral conventions.

The tanka reform movement of the *Myōjō* group took a remarkable step forward when it introduced a brilliant young poet who fervently pursued the tenets of romanticism in both her poetry and her life. The poet, who later married Tekkan and became known as Yosano Akiko (1878–1942), demonstrated in a dramatic way how the ideal of individualism could be translated into the ideal of romantic love, a type of love that feudal society did its best to suppress. In her late adolescence she fell passionately in love with Tekkan. Having accepted the strength of her feelings, she had no hesitation in leaving home to live with her lover, although he was a married man. *Midaregami* (Tangled Hair), her first collection of poetry, records the full range of emotion she experienced during those turbulent months. In many of the poems her most intimate desires are not only captured but welcomed. Such a bold affirmation of sensual love, especially coming from a young woman, at once shocked and fascinated contemporary readers, who in any case had to recognize her enormous poetic talent. In later years Akiko herself came to disapprove of some poems in *Midaregami*, but by that time she was well established as the foremost writer of love poetry in modern Japan.

Akiko's success made *Myōjō* the most influential po-
etry magazine in the first few years of the twentieth
century, almost completely overshadowing the works of
poets who belonged to older schools. Ironically, the
leader of her group also was a victim of this success, for
while Tekkan was pleased with the popularity of *Myōjō*,
his own poetic work looked rather pale in comparison
with that of Akiko, whom he had married in 1901. To be
sure, their passionate love affair had helped to expand
the scope of his poetry, which in earlier years had tended
to be nationalistic in theme and grandiose in style. Yet
many of his love poems were lacking in the brilliance,
boldness, and sensuality that characterized his wife's
tanka. He knew it himself, and the knowledge seems to
have made him rather excessively self-conscious in later
years. It might be said, however, that this very self-con-
sciousness has come to add a touch of modernity to his
later tanka and so given them a peculiar charm for to-
day's readers.

The Shasei Movement

Another group of young poets intent on tanka reform
gathered around Masaoka Shiki (1867–1902), a charis-
matic leader of the haiku modernization movement who
also had an active interest in tanka. Like Tekkan, Shiki
had feared that the kind of lifeless poetry currently being
written in thirty-one syllables exposed the form to the
danger of extinction, but in conceiving a way to reform it
he went in a direction radically different from the roman-
tics. The method he proposed was to utilize the principle
of *shasei*, or "sketch from life," which he had developed
in the course of his earlier attempt to reform haiku. In
his opinion, a poem expressive of the poet's self tended
to be commonplace and trite unless that self was highly
individualized, whereas a poem that faithfully observed
life was always fresh because people's lives were never

the same. Shiki voiced this opinion in a series of essays in 1898, attacking ancient and modern poems that seemed woefully deficient in fresh emotion. He and his group also began publishing an objective, descriptive type of tanka that depended more on observation than on imagination.

The shasei movement made little impact on the tanka scene during Shiki's lifetime, since his group had neither a group magazine like *Myōjō* nor a colorful advocate like Yosano Akiko. Shiki's disciples, however, not only remained unwavering in their faith in the shasei principle but attempted to cultivate it in a way more fitting to their own individual talents. Fortunately for them, people's fascination with romanticism rapidly waned a few years after the turn of the century and came to be replaced by an enthusiasm for the naturalistic realism that had been newly imported from the West. Encouraged, Shiki's followers began to publish several magazines. One such, founded in 1908 and called *Araragi* (The Yew Tree), especially gained popularity and in time became the most prestigious tanka magazine in the country. *Myōjō* expired two months after the founding of *Araragi*.

The *Araragi* group could boast a good number of gifted poets among its members, but the one who contributed most to the modernization of tanka was Saitō Mokichi (1882–1953). Ardent follower of Shiki as he was, young Mokichi was also associated with members of other schools such as the *Myōjō* group and gradually developed a theory of shasei that was uniquely his own. The knowledge of Western psychological aesthetics, which he absorbed while he was in Europe for professional training in psychiatry, also helped him in formulating the theory. In contrast to Shiki, to whom the life to be sketched in poetry had by and large meant external, visual life, Mokichi believed in portraying a life force that was at once psychic and biological: "To penetrate into the true aspect [of the subject] and sketch life that is a union of nature and the self—that is what shasei means." To Mokichi, the poet's subject matter was not just external but internal, because fidelity to it was possible only when external nature and the internal self merged in one. Such an idea of artistic representation seems to place Mokichi distinctly apart from naturalistic realism, and indeed his poetry gains much of its charm from the powerful language in which he gave vent to his own emotions. Interestingly, in seeking a strong lyrical precedent he went beyond Western literature and discovered it in the ancient Japanese poetry collected in *Man'yōshū*. Throughout his career Mokichi was a controversialist who fiercely defended the stand of the *Araragi* group, yet his own poetic theory and practice include a great deal more.

Another major poet who made his tanka debut in the pages of *Araragi* was Shaku Chōkū (1887–1953), whose main career was that of an ethnologist under his real name, Orikuchi Shinobu. His poems began appearing in *Araragi* in 1909, and a few years later he became one of the editors who screened other poets' tanka for publication in that magazine. Yet his talent as poet was too strongly individualistic to tie him to any group, and he knew it. He left the *Araragi* group in 1921 and began devoting himself to writing poetry that would allow full play to his personal interests. Central among these was a search for primordial human nature, a search that he believed should involve tracing the roots of folklore and uncovering the cultural legacies of the ancients. His typical poems present human emotions that hark back to the primeval, and they do so in a vocabulary that sounds even more archaic than *Man'yōshū*, although readers always feel the presence of a modern poet. His tanka are not romantic poems that long for the simple beauty of primitive culture; rather, they focus on the pathos of the human condition, unchanged for millennia of time. Chōkū skillfully expressed that pathos, not through the hackneyed vocabulary of the courtly waka tradition, but in the language of common people far removed from the urban civilization of twentieth-century Japan.

Tanka as Social Criticism

A third group of reformers also subscribed to the shasei principle, but they attached a different meaning to the "life" that was to be the subject of their "sketches." Whereas Mokichi and Chōkū associated life with the poet's subjective self, these poets wanted to see it as social reality outside the individual. To them, shasei meant portraying society as it really was, thereby revealing the pitfalls that lay in wait for the ordinary person. This idea was encouraged both by naturalistic literary theories imported from Europe and by the social situation in Japan, which had begun to show the ills of a modern industrial society.

The most notable member of the group was Ishikawa Takuboku (1886–1912), though his fame came only after his tormented life ended in premature death. The prime cause of his tragedy lay in his youthful overestimation of the usefulness of poetry in the everyday world. Endowed with ample poetic talent but with little practical ability, young Takuboku had a hard time earning a livelihood for himself and his family. He began blaming the structure of contemporary society, which he thought catered largely to the interests of a privileged class. Gradually he was converted to a belief in social reform and came to see the use of poetry from that angle. A poet was not to be a loner who leisurely jotted down whatever came to mind. "In our age," Takuboku said, "everyone must be a member of society and engage himself in a great deal of struggle." His later tanka can be read as records of that struggle. As such, they were distinctly different from premodern waka, which in general had little to do with social criticism. Takuboku wanted to indicate the difference visually. Instead of writing a tanka in one continuous line as had been the custom, he published his in three lines while keeping the 5–7–5–7–7 syllable pattern intact. On the printed page, his tanka looked like short free verse.

Actually, three-line tanka was an invention not of Takuboku but of his friend, Toki Zenmaro (1885–1980). A bold experimenter throughout his long career, Zenmaro explored the possibilities of the tanka form more thoroughly than most other poets. His first book of tanka, published in 1910, shocked readers because all the poems in it were written not only in three lines but in Roman letters. A magazine he founded three years later, *Seikatsu to geijutsu* (Life and Art), promoted the literature of social protest, often publishing the works of socialists blacklisted by the government. In the early 1930s, he joined a movement for writing "free-style tanka," that is, tanka unrestricted by syllable count. In the late 1950s he advocated "epic tanka" and himself wrote many poems on ancient Japanese historical figures. Despite all these experiments, however, Zenmaro's tanka consistently reveal the keen perception of a man who believes human society could, and should, be better than it is. He was a journalist by profession, and it shows in his poetry. Compared with Takuboku, he had more common sense and a better understanding of people who were not poets. His poetry may not be as powerfully lyrical as Takuboku's, but the message it contains is often more firmly rooted in reality.

The multiline tanka of Takuboku and the young Zenmaro encouraged some other radical poets to experiment with "free-style tanka." To those poets, all efforts at modernization were bound to fall short until the form and language of tanka were modernized and brought closer to the reality of contemporary society. Thus they wanted tanka to adopt not only the vocabulary of common speech but also its rhythms, which naturally did not

follow any predetermined syllable pattern. In 1925 the
radicals gathered together to found an organization
called the New Tanka Society. The society attracted a
number of young left-wing poets and became a conspicu-
ous part of the poetic landscape in Japan for a short
period of time.

Tanka by Writers of Fiction

Tanka reform was also aided by some authors who wrote
thirty-one-syllable poetry as their secondary form of liter-
ary expression. They include two prominent writers of
prose fiction, Mori Ōgai (1862–1922) and Okamoto Ka-
noko (1889–1939). Neither of the two was a member of
the reform groups, but both lived in Europe for a time
and their experiences in the West helped them bring
nontraditional qualities to their waka.

Curiously enough, Ōgai began his poetic career in
earnest while he was on active service during the Russo-
Japanese War. Apparently, writing poetry provided him
with relief of tension as well as a handy substitute for
keeping a diary. Back in Japan after the war, he hosted
tanka-writing parties to which he invited members of
both the *Myōjō* and *Araragi* groups. "I wanted to bring
the two closer together," he confided later. His
peacemaking attempt led nowhere, yet the parties gave
him plenty of stimulation to write poetry himself. Ōgai's
tanka are varied in style, ranging widely between the two
extremes of *Myōjō* and *Araragi* and yet always showing
his rare powers of observation and analysis. Today, his
poetry is almost completely overshadowed by the reputa-
tion of his fiction, but because his tanka are more sponta-
neous they provide some useful insights into the great
mind of that reserved, stoic novelist.

The tanka of Okamoto Kanoko are even less known
today, despite the fact that they number over four thou-
sand. Kanoko herself emphasized the important position

they occupied in her life, intimating, in an often-quoted comment, that she was a camel with three humps: tanka, prose fiction, and religion. Her emphasis notwithstanding, it has generally been felt that many of her tanka look amateurish, that they have not benefited from the considerable gift for literary craftsmanship that is manifest in her prose fiction. It might be argued, however, that that craftsmanship was obtained—at least partly— through her experience in writing tanka, an experience that preceded her career as a novelist. Her poems treat major themes of her prose fiction, too, albeit in a more fragmentary form. Above all they celebrate female sexuality, somewhat in the vein of Yosano Akiko. But Kanoko was also concerned with the often tragic consequences of intense passion and desire, and that concern took on religious overtones in her later writings. Her interest in Buddhism, evident in her prose works, reveals itself to varying degrees in her poems. Her tanka may not show the artistry of her fiction, but they do present more vividly the complex mind of a modern Japanese woman trying to live her life as fully as possible.

Tanka by Free-Verse Poets

New types of tanka were also written by poets primarily known for their works in free verse. Historically, modern Japanese free verse originated in *shintaishi*, or "new-style poetry," which was devised in the late nineteenth century as a way of translating Western poetry. Unlike tanka or haiku, shintaishi had no limit on the total number of syllables, although it still followed the traditional pattern of five- and seven-syllable units. The new verse form was attractive to many poets who had become disillusioned with older forms, and even such poets as Tekkan, Shiki, and Takuboku, who still had hopes for tanka, tried their hands at shintaishi. Then, as time passed and poets were more exposed to Western poetry, they became less happy with the syllable scheme of shintaishi and began writing poems that were not restricted by it. The first notable book of free verse was published in 1907. Since then, free verse has come to dominate Japanese poetry outside of tanka and haiku.

A major poet in the early years of free verse was Kitahara Hakushū (1885–1942), whose first two books of poetry received lavish praise for their display of an extraordinarily delicate, somewhat decadent sensibility as well as for their brilliantly colorful language and strikingly exotic imagery. These features had been derived from French symbolist poetry, of which he was an avid reader. Thus when he brought out his first collection of tanka in 1913, readers discovered similar poetic qualities in it and were impressed by its novelty. Hakushū himself, comparing tanka poetry to a precious stone, commented: "I wanted to add a new tinge of French symbolism to that old green gem." Interestingly, as he grew older he became more attracted to the kind of Japanese symbolism found in *Shin kokinshū*. In his later years, he seems to have discarded even that type of symbolism in favor of the simplicity and plainness that characterize haiku and Zen poetry. Not surprisingly, the older Hakushū wrote more tanka and less free verse.

The case of Miyazawa Kenji (1896–1932) is very different. He wrote some one thousand tanka in his youth. At the age of twenty-five, however, he was awakened to the charms of free verse and abandoned the thirty-one-syllable form almost completely. His later works in free verse are so dazzling that few take the trouble of reading his tanka today. But the tanka are interesting for the light they throw on the Sturm und Drang of Kenji's early life. Scattered throughout them are fragments of his unique cosmology, founded on the Lotus sect of Buddhism as well as on Western geological science, together with other thoughts that crossed his unsettled, morbidly sensitive young mind. Although he began writing tanka under

Takuboku's influence, the poetic reality he wanted to present in them was more cosmic and visionary than his mentor's. The dominating imagery in his tanka is more like that seen in the modernist poetry of later years. He was ahead of his time in tanka, just as he was in free verse.

The Left-Wing Tanka Movement

The severe economic depression that swept Japan after World War I, coupled with the news of the successful Russian Revolution, gave rise to a left-wing movement in many segments of Japanese society. Literature could not remain unaffected. The first literary magazine that promoted socialism appeared in 1921 and was followed immediately by several more. The League of Japanese Proletarian Writers was formed in 1925; the following year it expanded to become the League of Proletarian Artists. Left-wing tanka poets were somewhat late in organizing themselves, but finally in 1928 they banded together to form the League of Rising Tanka Poets, which was reorganized as the League of Proletarian Tanka Poets a few months later. Their immediate goal was to renounce the existing tradition of tanka, which in their view implicitly supported the continuation of the bourgeoisie, and to replace it with a new type of tanka rooted in the lives of proletarians. New tanka, they felt, should present the plight of laborers and express their desire for social change. In form, they favored vernacular, free-style tanka, which they considered closer to the language of common people.

In retrospect, it has to be said that the left-wing tanka movement suffered the same fate as similar movements in other literary genres. The poets who participated in it were so eager to articulate their ideology that their poems tended to be lacking in craftsmanship and emotional appeal. In their eagerness to pursue their political ideals, they did not pay enough attention to their personal feelings. In this respect, they were not unlike those waka poets before the reform who merely imitated conventional emotions contained in famous poems of earlier times. To be sure, the leftists' tanka looked different from traditional waka since they wrote in a form free from syllabic restrictions. Yet they were not convincing in their explanations as to why their poems had to be called tanka and not free verse. By its very nature, then, left-wing tanka was under a handicap, and the increasing government repression did not help either. The League of Proletarian Tanka Poets disbanded in 1932, only two and a half years after its establishment. The popularity of free-style tanka also declined rapidly.

Many of the left-wing tanka that still retain some appeal today are the work of poets who were not too firmly committed to the movement. The case of Ōkuma Nobuyuki (1893–1977) is typical. As a young man Nobuyuki was a leftist sympathizer and helped to organize the League of Rising Tanka Poets, himself writing a number of poignant tanka showing concern with social problems from a socialist point of view. Yet his concern was more humanitarian than ideological, and when the proletarian tanka movement became distinctly political, he parted ways with his comrades. He did retain the leftists' predilection for writing tanka with no syllabic restrictions, and later tried to defend the practice by theorizing that free-style tanka is different from free verse because it has a unique "fixed quantity." In his view, ordinary tanka has both the fixed form roughly structured on a 5–7–5–7–7 pattern and the fixed quantity roughly measured by the total of thirty-one syllables. Free-style tanka, he theorized, disregards the fixed form but retains the fixed quantity; therefore it is not free verse. It is not clear how seriously Nobuyuki was committed to this defense, for after a few years he seemed to abandon any attempt to approximate the tanka form, writing many poems in free verse instead.

After 1937, he became a full-time scholar specializing in economics and stopped writing poetry altogether.

The Modernists

The left-wing movement had the effect of polarizing the contemporary tanka scene, for it pushed poets of the opposing camp farther in the direction of "pure" poetry devoid of political and social implications. Poets in this latter camp were known as "modernists" because, like their namesakes in Europe, they had a belief in art for art's sake, a desire to escape from the sordid reality of life, and a preference for surrealist imagery and symbolic language. In their opinion, no tanka of high artistic quality was likely to be born from commonplace emotions of ordinary people expressed in the vernacular. Poetry, they insisted, should address itself not just to existing social reality but to universal human experience. What they wanted to do was engage in a quest for transcendental truth, and to articulate the results through images and symbols that went beyond the logic of ordinary thinking. Whether they succeeded in that attempt is open to debate, but it seems beyond dispute that the best of their tanka are more readable today than anything written by the left-wing movement.

In 1930 some of the modernists gathered together to form the Art School Tanka Club. Although the club itself did not last long, its principal organizer, Maekawa Samio (1903–1990), became the antiproletarian poets' standard-bearer because of the plaudits his first book of tanka, *Shokubutsusai* (The Rite of the Plants), received upon its publication in 1930. His early poetry often displays youthful aspiration for unattainable ideals and the resultant pain and despair, which are expressed in arcane language and enigmatic imagery. His language grew a little more realistic in his later poetry, but his longing for the unearthly remained by and large unchanged. "Tanka is never to be found in struggles with muddy reality," he wrote when he was forty-eight. "It lies in abstracted emotion with no visible form or shape, and makes the kind of soughing sound that an angel's wings would make in the wind." Still, with all his enthusiasm for such free flight of the soul, he was not tempted to write free-style tanka. He tried to use the conventional closed form to create tension with what it enclosed, and he was successful in that attempt to a remarkable degree.

Another major figure in the modernist camp was Saitō Fumi (b. 1909), who made her poetic debut with Samio's help. Her tanka, like the older poet's, are filled with surrealistic images that suggest her persistent search for ideals that lie beyond mundane reality. She once intimated that by writing tanka she had been trying to present "something that is sparkling beyond the reach of language and yet accessible through human sensibility." Yet, in contrast to Samio, who liked to compare a poet to a bird aspiring to fly up to heaven, Fumi's first book of poetry was entitled *Gyoka* (Songs of a Fish), suggesting that she felt more like a fish struggling under the enormous weight of water or against a strong current. Beneath its colorful surface, her poetry contains dark emotions arising from protracted suffering, abysmal despair, and wish for the peace of death. In his preface to *Gyoka*, Samio predicted she would become the first major woman poet since Yosano Akiko. She proved the prediction right, but by exploring an area of tanka distinctly different from Akiko's.

World War II and Its Aftermath

Few literary masterpieces were produced in the years between the 1937 Marco Polo Bridge Incident and Japan's defeat in World War II, as the wartime government severely curtailed freedom of speech. Tanka was not as severely repressed as many other literary genres, because its premodern predecessor, waka, had for centuries been associated with the imperial court and with the samurai class. Under the government's leadership, one hundred patriotic waka by one hundred poets were selected and recommended for use in a traditional game children played at New Year's. Some prominent tanka poets, such as Saitō Mokichi and Maekawa Samio, willingly wrote poems promoting nationalism and the prowar spirit. A few, like Shaku Chōkū and Toki Zenmaro, dared to publish tanka with antiwar implications, but even they fell silent or wrote passively cooperative poems as the war progressed and repression intensified.

The end of the war in 1945 brought utter confusion to the defeated nation and its people. To poets and writers, however, it meant the beginning of an era that allowed them to write whatever they wanted to write. Those who shared similar literary goals organized themselves into groups and founded magazines through which to disseminate their views. Tanka poets with left-wing inclinations founded *Jinmin tanka* (People's Tanka) six months after the end of the war. The *Araragi* group, which had suspended the magazine in 1944, resumed publication at about the same time. Poets who were more romantically inclined gathered together to revive *Myōjō* in 1947. There was also a new generation of poets who were dissatisfied with most of the theories and practices of prewar poets. They founded the Society of New Tanka Poets in late 1946 and began exchanging ideas as to how they could create tanka that would reflect the radically new society beginning to emerge in the war's aftermath. It was this last group of poets that came to produce some of the best works of the postwar period and set the pace for tanka poets in the second half of the twentieth century.

One of the two leading members of the society was Kondō Yoshimi (b. 1913), even though he had been associated with the *Araragi* group in his youth and had had his early poems published in that magazine. Like the mainstream *Araragi* poets, he had faith in shasei as a principle of tanka composition. Unlike them, however, he believed that the subject matter of poetry should reflect the poet's desire for social change. "If our realism meant nothing more than copying life as it is, the resulting picture would seem too dark," he said. "We must look at 'reality as it should be' while looking at 'reality as it is.'" For Yoshimi, "reality as it should be" had clearly political implications, because, as a soldier drafted and forced to fight during the war, he was painfully aware of the enormous power a government has over the lives of those whom it governs. In his view, no poet could portray life without being conscious of the contemporary political situation. Thus his tanka freely treat such subjects as the atomic bomb, the Korean War, the U.S.-Japan Mutual Security Treaty, and the Vietnam War—all observed through the eyes of a concerned intellectual who firmly believes man is capable of creating a better world by political means.

The other prominent member of the Society of New Tanka Poets was Miya Shūji (1911–1986), who went in a direction different from Yoshimi in his search for innovation in postwar tanka. Whereas his younger colleague looked to political power as a vehicle for social change, Shūji had little or no faith in government, probably because his experience as a soldier on the battlefield was even more devastating than Yoshimi's. In 1949 he declared himself a "loner" and explained: "All orders are issued by those who have never been wounded by change—in other words, by those who can change without being hurt, who feel no regret or shame after the change. . . . I no longer have faith in orders coming from them." His distrust of government did not mean disinterest in politics or society, and he went on to write a number of tanka on such current topics as the 1964 Tokyo Olympics, the Soviet invasion of Hungary, and the revolutions in Iraq, from a viewpoint free from political ideologies. Yet it cannot be denied that he came to pay greater attention to his personal life, and the forces sustaining that life from within, as the war grew more remote in time. This tendency was especially pronounced in the works of his last ten years, when he suffered from various illnesses. He had begun writing tanka under Kitahara Hakushū, but his later poetry is closer to some of the finest poems written by *Araragi* poets.

Avant-Garde Tanka

"Avant-garde tanka" is a name given by the mass media, but lack of a better term has caused it to be widely used to designate the works of certain young poets who, with their striking imagery and bold technique, shocked general readers of tanka in the mid-1950s. The movement can be seen as a revival of modernism, which had been at a low ebb in the postwar period due to lack of leadership. Yet the new poets also showed definite signs of belonging to the postwar generation. Their tanka were less lyrical than the modernists'. They seemed more socially conscious. They also tended to be more intellectual in technique, more ironic in tone, and more abstruse in expression.

Those traits are clearly seen in the works of Tsukamoto Kunio (b. 1922), who is generally considered the most influential figure among the poets associated with avant-garde tanka. He advocated "the realism of the soul" in tanka composition and asked: "What mission could a short fixed verse form like tanka have except to present visions?" His poetry is indeed filled with visionary images seen by his mind's eye. Yet his visions are not segments of a harmonious world; rather they suggest a chaotic cosmos whose components are not at ease with one another. As haiku poets often do, he takes advantage of the short fixed form by presenting mutually conflicting images and thereby creating a striking comparison or contrast. In this sense his poetry might be called imagist tanka, yet that designation is not quite adequate because he often adds to it the waka technique of classical allusion. The meaning of his poems is often enriched by ironic allusion to the cultural heritage of Japan and the West, in both of which he is immensely learned.

There is some controversy as to whether the works of Nakajō Fumiko (1922–1954) fall within the boundaries of avant-garde tanka, yet there is no doubt that they were as boldly radical and had as striking an impact on the mid-century tanka scene. Her boldness as a tanka poet had existential roots: during the period that she wrote her most beautiful tanka, she knew she was dying of breast cancer. Her life before this fatal illness had been unfortunate enough. Her girlhood had coincided with the dark years of the war. Her marriage broke up because of her husband's drinking and drug addiction. A young man she fell in love with after the divorce died of tuberculosis. Somehow she found the courage to survive all these previous misfortunes, but she had a hard time coping with the cancer. "When I was confronted with the terror of the incurable disease," she said, "I was for the first time convinced of my doom, and that conviction enabled my hands to reach life at the deepest level." She took the power she obtained and made it into tanka. She was comfortable with the tanka form because she felt its syllabic confinement matched the confined life she was living in a cancer ward. By expressing what lay at the basis of her life, she turned tanka into a weapon against the terror of death. For Fumiko, who believed in no religion, tanka was her light and her salvation.

Tanka in Japan Today

In today's Japan, tanka seems to be thriving as ever. In addition to the two major tanka magazines that have

been published since the postwar period, a third was
founded in 1977, and a fourth in 1987. Furthermore,
several hundred "little magazines" are published by tanka
groups scattered all over the country. In 1979 and 1980 a
major commercial publisher brought out twenty volumes
of *Shōwa Man'yōshū* (*Man'yōshū* of the Shōwa Era),
anthologizing some 50,000 tanka written during the reign
of Emperor Shōwa. Another large publishing house is-
sued the fifteen-volume *Gendai tanka zenshū* (The
Grand Collection of Modern Tanka) in 1980 and 1981,
making available virtually all the major books of tanka
published in the last one hundred years. Then in 1987
Sarada kinenbi (Salad Anniversary), a slim volume of
tanka composed by a young high school teacher, became
a great bestseller, selling some two million copies within
six months. Even when a major earthquake killed some
5,000 people and destroyed more than 95,000 homes in
the Kobe area in 1995, sixty-eight local poets who escaped
serious injury transformed their harrowing experience
into a collection of over four hundred tanka and pub-
lished it under the title *Gareki no machi kara* (From the
Town of Rubble) only three months after the disaster. It
is generally believed that the popularity of literature has
been dwindling in Japan in the last several decades, but
that does not seem to be the case as far as tanka is
concerned.

From among many gifted poets writing tanka today,
two have been selected for this anthology: Sasaki Yuki-
tsuna (b. 1938) and Tawara Machi (b. 1962). Having
grown up in the late 1950s, which were the heyday of the
student peace movement, Yukitsuna began his career as
a representative of the "angry young men." He was
against the establishment in tanka as well as in other
matters, dissatisfied as he was with both the uncommitted
attitude of the shasei realists and the elitism of the art
school poets. When still an undergraduate, he declared:
"Don't let tanka fall into the possession of the defeated.

We must do the elementary but fundamental work of affirming humanity with rigor and singing the health of man with passion." His tanka are lively, unsentimental, and affirmative, calling out to mankind in a manly, sonorous language. For those traits, his tanka has been given a rather misleading label, *otoko uta* or "masculine poetry."

Otoko uta is a misleading label because Yukitsuna has a number of female followers who emulate him and whose works share the qualities of his tanka to varying degrees. The most prominent of them is Tawara Machi, author of the bestselling *Sarada kinenbi* mentioned above. Her tanka also affirm humanity and celebrate its positive aspects, but they do so by using a subject matter and language more familiar to ordinary readers than do Yukitsuna's works. Explaining her goal as a poet, she once said: "Something like a 'mood' wavers in our daily routines, like shopping, cooking and doing laundry. I want to put my hand gently on it and capture it intact. If I also capture the spirit of the age, so much the better." Those words suggest why her tanka are often characterized as being "light," in both the positive and the negative sense of the term. Her detractors equate the lightness with superficiality, charging that her poems merely present a mood that floats around the subject without ever trying to penetrate or analyze it. Her defenders, on the other hand, see in her lightness something of the younger generation's attitude that all serious analyses of life are in the end futile and useless. Obviously there have been far more defenders than detractors, for *Sarada kinenbi* has not only gained millions of readers but been made into a musical revue, a serial TV drama, and a full-length commercial movie. Its social impact has been so pervasive that a new phrase, "the Tawara phenomenon," was coined to describe it.

The great popularity of *Sarada kinenbi* is all the more remarkable in view of the fact that the death of tanka had been predicted by a number of prominent literary figures during the last one hundred years. The predictions seemed especially convincing in the late nineteenth century, when masterpieces of Western poetry were introduced to Japan, and again after World War II, when antitraditionalist feelings swept the country. Even among the tanka poets, Masaoka Shiki and Shaku Chōkū forecast an early death for the thirty-one-syllable form; Miyazawa Kenji abandoned tanka to become a free-verse poet; and Ōkuma Nobuyuki, together with many proletarian poets, wrote free-style tanka that were, in most readers' eyes, no different from free verse. The other major traditional verse form, the seventeen-syllable haiku, fared better in this respect because it was felt to be a more modern type of poetry—one that, by presenting images, allowed readers to take an active part in the act of reading. One wonders, then, how tanka has been able to survive the turbulent years of Japan's modern century. What are the charms of the age-old thirty-one-syllable form in the eyes of today's poets and readers, who lead a life completely different from that of the *Kokinshū* poets?

There is no simple answer to that question, as different people have found different charms in the tanka form. To observe a few examples from among the living poets, Kondō Yoshimi, an architect, seems to have been attracted to the simple beauty of the 5-7-5-7-7 syllable pattern. After voicing his distaste for the gaudy ornaments of a hearse, he says: "What we [tanka poets] consider beautiful is the simple beauty of modern architecture . . . the beauty of a form science pushed to its limits." By contrast, Tsukamoto Kunio is interested in the tanka form precisely because it is premodern and so contains a beauty and order that have been lost in the modern age. His tanka are created, he says, in the process of his effort to recapture the missing beauty and order and, by utilizing the power of suggestion inherent in the form, to elevate it to a new height. Sasaki Yukitsuna is also concerned with the ailments of the modern age, especially with the way in which language has become estranged from the things it is supposed to designate. He writes tanka, he says, because he believes that the age-old verse form is basically poetic speech in the first person, speech that may still be capable of overcoming that estrangement. For Tawara Machi, the main appeal of tanka is more functional than philosophical. She considers the predetermined verse form a "net" that filters the disorder of experience. She enjoys the tension she feels as her net scoops up the essentials and leaves out the rest. Many other explanations are given by today's poets regarding the charms of tanka, with no seeming consensus among them.

Perhaps this very lack of consensus is the best answer explaining why the ancient verse form is still strong. The tanka form is fixed and yet flexible. It provides a ready-made form so that poets need not worry about the shape of their verbal utterance, and yet the form is so pliant that they can bend it almost in any way they like. Furthermore, the form is rich in its cultural legacy: it has absorbed the essentials of Japanese civilization for the last 1,300 years and has established itself as the archetypal mode of emotional expression for those who speak Japanese. Because it is the archetypal mode, it touches and moves the Japanese heart at the deepest level. Some people in modern Japan dislike tanka and predict its extinction, but they do so precisely because the form is part of themselves and cannot cast aside. Tanka will continue to be written as long as Japanese culture continues to survive. A more pertinent question may be whether the tanka form is universal enough to be transplanted into a foreign soil and grow as vigorously as haiku. Having read some recent examples of English tanka, I am inclined to believe it is.

Modern

Japanese

Tanka

Yosano Tekkan

Son of a Buddhist priest, Yosano Tekkan was expected to become a preacher like his father and received some preparatory training as a child. He never fulfilled that expectation, but instead became a tireless and successful advocate for tanka reform. Today, he is remembered more for his activities as a reformer of tanka than for his poetry as such.

Tekkan was born Yosano Hiroshi on February 26, 1873, at a Buddhist temple in Kyoto. The temple, however, was closed down five years later, and the ensuing poverty forced the family to disperse. The young Tekkan had to work at various times as an acolyte, a schoolteacher, a journalist, and an editor, even making several trips to Korea in search of career opportunities. His activities gradually gained a focus as his poems and essays received recognition, and with the publication of his first two books of poetry in 1896 and 1897, he established himself as a standard-bearer of the tanka reform movement. Encouraged, he founded the magazine *Myōjō* in 1900, which quickly became the stronghold of romanticism. As its editor, Tekkan helped a number of gifted poets to make their literary debuts. In 1901 he married one of them, Akiko, after obtaining a divorce from his second wife.

The first several years of the twentieth century were the happiest period of Tekkan's career. Eventually, though, his reputation was surpassed by his wife's. His personal life, complicated by his three successive marriages, was treated as a scandal by the media. The most severe blow, however, was the rise of naturalistic realism on the Japanese literary scene. *Myōjō* was forced to suspend publication in 1908. Tekkan, trying to make a fresh start as a poet, began to write under his real name, Hiroshi, but he was never able to turn back the tide. His poetic production dwindled rapidly, and even a tour of Europe in 1912 did not help to recharge his creative energies. After being appointed a professor of Japanese at Keio University in 1919, he spent more energy as an educator than a poet. He died in Tokyo on March 26, 1935.

let those grasses
growing in the field
speak out
they will have tears to shed
they will have songs to sing

To our baby that died[1]

in the dark woods
lying ahead on your road
whom will you call?
you don't yet know the names
of your parents or your own

YOSANO TEKKAN   3

[1] Tekkan's daughter Fukiko died six weeks after birth in 1899.

*no ni ouru, kusa ni mo mono wo, iwase baya. namida mo aramu, uta
mo aramu.*

*shide no yama kuraki anata ni tare wo yobu oya no na mo shirazu
ono ga na mo shirazu*

too emotional
hence his brittle love
too talented
hence his eccentric verse
take pity on this poor man!

vast wilderness
on the African continent
and my stubbornness
both from the primeval age
something beautiful in common

nasake sugite koi mina moroku sai amarite uta mina ki nari ware wo awareme

Afurika no taiya to ware no katakuna to kono furuki mono yoku utsukushiki

I'll forget I saw you
standing with a stupified look
hands holding your breasts
when an earthquake shook this morning
so bring me a drink, my dear

in my mind
suddenly it appeared
then passed away
the black barge with neither
a window nor a light

nai no asa munaji idakeru akiregao miki to wa iwaji sake seyo tojime

*waga uchi ni tsuto yuki kienu mado mo naku tomoshibi mo naki
kuroki hakobune*

with warts and all
the true image of a toad
vividly emerges
from those popular poems
rare treasures of our time [2]

their father
strikes them again and again
their mother
screams she wants a divorce
pitiful children of ours

YOSANO TEKKAN

[2] Written in 1908, when naturalistic realism began to dominate the Japanese literary scene.

ibo arite gama no sugata wo itsuwarazu ware chinchō su ryūzoku no uta

sono chichi wa uchi chōchaku su sono haha wa wakaremu to iu awarenaru kora

poppies in bloom
bring back to memory
those lips I kissed
while lying in an attic
lit up with the evening sun

Snake
Fox, Arsonist, Thief
Kidnapper
somehow they call me
by those unusual names

*keshi sakinu omou wa hikuki yaneura no yūyake ni nete suishi
kuchibiru*

*hebi kitsune hitsuke nusubito kadowakashi okashiki na nomi ware wa
morainu*

the bliss
of a chicken taking a bath
in the dirt
willingly I too stand
in the dust of disdain

plucking feathers
from a white swan
placed on the lap
the phantom of a person
mirrored in my eyes

niwatori no suna wo ba aburu kokoroyosa ware mo motomete azakeri
wo abu

hiza no ue ni shiratori no ha wo mushiri inu waga me ni utsuru
maboroshi no hito

faintly white
as the eyes open
on my soul
trying to escape
through an old window

eyes fixed
on the neck of a camel
standing immobile
I too wait calmly
for the arrival of my time

YOSANO TEKKAN   9

usujiroku waga tamashii wa me wo akinu furuki mado yori nogaren to shite

ugokazaru rakuda no kubi wo mitsume tsutsu ware mo shizukani waga toki wo matsu

not unlike a fish
in the depths of water
listening to the bubbles
that rise to the surface
this weary soul of mine

with no flower buds
this vine continues to climb
straight upwards
intent on blooming nowhere
save in the heavens

*tsubutsubu to awadatsu mizu wo soko ni kiku uo no tagui ka umeru
tamashii*

*mizukara no hana wo oshimeru kono tsuru wa sora ni sakan to yoji
nobori yuku*

except the rare time
when it overflows its banks
this river here
is mostly dry, with many
unsightly rocks exposed

it cries and cries
loud, long and shamelessly
not knowing
the art of the shorter poem
a cicada

afururu wa tadani hitotoki ōkata wa minikuki ishi wo arawaseru nari

naki ni naku asamashi nagashi kashigamashi mijikaki uta wo shiranu
semi kana

unlike their father
what happy careers are in store
for all my children
who show absolutely no fear
of algebra or a dog

noiselessly
a group of black-robed nuns
walked by
leaving nothing behind
except the evening glow

chichi ni ninu koto mo tanomoshi kora wa mina daisūgaku to inu wo osorezu

oto mo naku kuroki koromo no amatachi ga sugitsuru ato ni nokoru yūyake

Masaoka Shiki

The pseudonym Shiki, by which Masaoka Tsunenori is widely known, refers to a small cuckoo-like bird that, according to a legend, keeps singing until it spits blood. Tsunenori adopted the name after he spat blood every night for a week in May 1889, when he was twenty-one years old. If tuberculosis had not struck him down, there might have been neither a poet named Shiki nor the poetry reforms he initiated, for his youthful ambition had been to become a statesman.

Shiki was born on October 14, 1867, in Matsuyama on the island of Shikoku. Because his father was a samurai and his maternal grandfather a Confucian scholar, he received a good training in Chinese classics as a child and began writing Chinese verse at age eleven. His earliest extant tanka was written when he was fifteen. In 1884 he obtained a scholarship and entered Tokyo University, but he was more interested in extracurricular activities, such as playing baseball and writing poetry, than in pursuing his studies. In 1892 he left the university without graduating and began working for the newspaper *Nippon*. His essays on haiku, published in the newspaper, started the haiku reform movement. When the Sino-Japanese War broke out in 1894 he traveled to China as a war correspondent, despite his doctor's advice not to do so. As had been feared, he coughed up blood on his way home and had to be hospitalized for a month after arriving back in Japan. For the next three years he wrote mostly haiku and promoted a new style of haiku based on the shasei principle. He did have a desire to initiate tanka reform, but apparently his superiors at the newspaper, many of whom wrote tanka themselves, were uneasy about his radical views and would not allow him to express them there. In 1898 he finally persuaded the editors of *Nippon* to let him publish a series of essays voicing the need for tanka reform. He also began holding tanka-writing parties at his home, although those who gathered there were mostly haiku poets at first. The majority of his tanka surviving today were written during the last five years of his life, when he was largely bedridden. He died on September 19, 1902. He had composed nearly 2,500 tanka in all, although no collection was published during his lifetime.

nobody with me
as spring prepares to depart
from my garden
leaving petals of the kerria
gathered on the water

During an illness

fresh new leaves
on a tiny weed in my yard
hinting at
the boundless space on earth
now filled with spring green

*hito mo kozu haru yuku niwa no mizu no ue ni koborete tamaru
yamabuki no hana*

*waga niwa no ogusa mo moenu kagiri naki ametsuchi ima ya midori
suru rashi*

peacefully
the hamlet is asleep
with all its lights out
the River of Heaven[1]
white above a bamboo grove

tree with lush leaves
at an outdoor fair
giving shade
to a goldfish seller
as summer begins

[1] *Amanogawa*, literally meaning "the river of heaven," refers to the Milky Way.

neshizumaru sato no tomoshibi mina kiete amanogawa shiroshi
takeyabu no ue ni

wakaba sasu ichi no ueki no shitakage ni kingyo akinau natsu wa
kinikeri

Among the poems I wrote
with many pictures spread
out before me[2]

under a tree
lies the Buddha, surrounded
by elephants
snakes and the like
all in tears

makes me writhe
in bed, this excruciating
pain of illness
alongside a tree peony
with its flowers open

MASAOKA SHIKI   17

[2] The specific picture this poem alludes to is *Nehan'e,* which portrays a scene of Buddha's death.

ki no moto ni fuseru hotoke wo uchikakomi zō hebidomo no naki iru tokoro

koimarobu yamai no toko no kurushimi no sono katawara ni botan saku nari

illuminated
in the light of a lamp
outside the window
a tree peony in the misty rain
this spring night

My room

butterbur
blooming in a small pot
alongside
volumes of haiku, tanka
dictionaries strewn about

18   MASAOKA SHIKI

*tomoshibi no hikari ni terasu mado no soto no botan ni sosogu haru
no yo no ame*

*fuki no hana ueshi kobachi no katawara ni torimidashitaru haisho
kasho jisho*

Upon receiving potted
peonies for a gift

placed
near the pillow
of my sickbed
a potted tree peony
its flowers swaying a while

A view of my garden

crimson-budded rose
grown to two feet tall
its thorns
tender in the misty
spring rain

*yami fuseru waga makurabe ni hakobi kuru hachi no botan no hana
yureyamazu*

*kurenai no nishaku nobitaru bara no me no hari yawarakani
harusame no furu*

During a trip

pink clover
blooming all over the field
next to
a filthy pond
with domestic ducks

The first of May[3]

kerria roses
are gone, mustard flowers
have turned to seeds
the first day of May
begins my month of doom

[3] Written on May 1, 1900. Shiki had first spat blood on May 9, 1889, and dreaded the coming of another May.

gengen no hana saku hara no katawara ni ahiru kaitaru kitanaki ike ari

yamabuki wa chiri na no hana wa mi ni narite gogatsu tsuitachi ware yaku ni iru

beyond the glass door
the bright rays of the moon
illuminating
above the grove of trees
a long trail of white cloud

in the vase
a plume of wisteria
hanging
too short to reach
the tatami floor

MASAOKA SHIKI   21

garasudo no to wa tsuki akashi mori no ue ni shirakumo nagaku tanabikeru miyu

bin ni sasu fuji no hanabusa mijikakereba tatami no ue ni todokazarikeri

dipped
into mellow sake wine
the withered flowers
of wisteria
come back to life again

the day I had in mind
for a tanka poets' party
has come and gone
now beginning to fall
flowers of the kerria

yashioori no sake ni hitaseba shioretaru fujinami no hana yomigaeri
saku

uta no kai hirakan to omou hi mo sugite chirigata ni naru yamabuki
no hana

hawkers
letter carriers and all
come and go
by my back door where
the kerria flowers bloom

on a young pine
long green shoots
this long day
my temperature rises
with the approaching night

*akindo mo fumikubaribito mo yukichigau urado no waki no yamabuki
no hana*

*wakamatsu no medachi no midori nagaki hi wo yū katamakete netsu
idenikeri*

in the house
no wind blows and yet
unable to resist
nature's law
plum blossoms fall

Having molded clay in the
shape of my ailing form

my departed soul
should it linger
in this world
would probably stay
around this lump of earth

*ie no uchi ni kaze wa fukanedo kotowari ni arasoikanete ume no chiru
ka mo*

*waga kokoro yo ni shi nokoraba aragane no kono tsuchikure no hotori
ni ka aran*

Mori Ōgai

Few would object to calling
Mori Ōgai a Renaissance man of early modern Japan.
He was trained in medicine and eventually came to
occupy the highest medical office in the military, yet his
achievements as novelist, critic, and translator were sec-
ond to none in his time. Consequently his tanka seems
almost like an insignificant byproduct of his distin-
guished career.

Ōgai, whose real name was Mori Rintarō, was born in
Shimane prefecture on February 17, 1862. Because his
father was a physician, he too prepared for a medical
career and studied medicine at Tokyo University, gradu-
ating in 1881. An ambitious young man, he wanted to go
to Europe for further study and so enlisted in the army,
which had an overseas study program. His wish was ful-
filled in 1884, when he was sent to Germany for four
years of medical training. Beside studying medicine, he
did extensive reading in literature, philosophy, and aes-
thetics while he was in Europe. These studies helped
him launch a secondary career as a translator and scholar
in the humanities after he returned to Japan in 1888 and
joined the faculty of the Army Medical College. His
double career was, however, interrupted when the army
sent him to China as a medical officer during both the
Sino-Japanese and the Russo-Japanese wars. It was during
the latter war that he began to keep a poetic diary.

Having learned the pleasure of writing tanka, he began
to hold verse-writing parties when he returned home after
the war. Tekkan, Akiko, Hakushū, Takuboku, Mokichi,

and many other prominent poets of the day attended at one time or another. From 1910 on, Ōgai's creative energy was directed more toward writing fiction, resulting in such famous works as *Gan* (The Wild Goose) and *Sanshō dayū* (Sanshō the Steward). In 1916 he retired from the army after thirty-five years of service, the last nine as surgeon-general. Yet his intelligence, erudition, and administrative ability were much in demand, and in his later years he served in such positions as director of the Imperial Museum and president of the Imperial Academy of Art. He died of lung and kidney ailments on July 9, 1922. He had married twice and had five children.

let a poem be
like a crystal bowl
filled with ice
delightfully transparent
leaving no spot invisible

under the blue sky
in a dewy cornfield
basking
in the morning sunlight
a caramel-colored cow

uta mo kakare kōri wo moreru hari no ban hogarani sukite mienu kuma naki

aozora no moto ni tsuyukeki kimibata ya asahi ami tatsu ameushi hitotsu

frolicking
over the scattered books
a little mouse
I pretend to be asleep
and watch it for a while

far and near
the sound of conches
along the seashore
the clamors of boatsmen
could there be whales coming?

*chiriboeru fumi no ue yuku konezumi wo netaru furi shite shibashi
mamorinu*

*ochi kochi ni kai no ne hibiki ura zutai funabito sawagu kujira yoru
rashi*

close by the host
seeing a guest to the gate
with lantern in hand
a branch of the cherry tree
blossoming in the dark night

on a post
near the edge of a brook
a crow
utterly still
in the stillness of high noon

hi wo torite marōdo okuru watadono ni hitoeda chikaki yami no yozakura

satogawa no kishibe no kui ni karasu ite mijirogi mo senu hiru no shizukesa

but for the dew
dripping from the flowers
of wisteria
the eye can catch nothing of
this rain in the evening dusk

during a break
in the long seasonal rain
winged ants hover
off the eaves of a shack
in the evening sunlight

*fujinami no hana no tsuyu nomi shitatarite furu to mo miezu tasogare
no ame*

*samidare no haretaru hima ni haari tatsu fuseya no noki no yūzuku
hi kana*

it will not be heard
by those living in the foothills
this evening bell
ringing at a mountain temple
buried under the young leaves

trying to perch
on the swaying flower
of a waterweed
in the middle of a brook
a butterfly dallies

*fumoto ni wa kikoezaruran yamadera no wakaba ni komoru iriai no
kane*

*satogawa no nagare ni yuragu mo no hana ni tomaran to shite chō no
izayou*

step by step
as I move forward on the wet ground
in the dark
my hands touch the gravestones
that mark the path

white swan
plowing through the waves
with its neck
perpendicularly erect
look how the head does not move!

*shimeritaru tsuchi wo ashi fumi yami ni tatsu haka yori haka ni te
furete yukinu*

*nami wo kiru kano shiratori no enchokuni tatetaru kubi no ugokazaru
miyo*

without incident
another day is gone
while I keep gazing
at the unidentifiable
color of the wall

should I stroke it
sparks will shoot up and scatter
from her black hair
that coils around my body
and keeps me tightly bound

hi hitohi kyō mo koto nashi komori ite nan tomo wakanu kabe no iro miru

kainadeba hibana chirubeki kurokami no nawa ni waga mi wa shibararete ari

your heart
still remains unsettled
like the wavering
of a cosmos flower
after the bee is gone

some medals
compensate for the terror
of the moment
while others pay for many
humdrum days spent in service

*mikokoro wa imada ochiizu hachi sarite kosumosu no kuki yurameku
gotoku*

kunshō wa jiji no kyōfu ni kaetaru to hibi no shōka ni kaetaru to ari

never have I
stopped to gaze at something
for long
my feet that tread on life
having been too healthy

an insane thought
flashes across my mind
like a fire
that suddenly flares up
in a city at night

nani hitotsu yoku wa mizariki sei wo fumu waga ashi amari sukuyaka nareba

kuruoshiki kangae ukabu yoru no machi ni futo moeizuru kaji no gotoku ni

In Nara (two poems)

did the people of Nara[1]
want to obliterate
autumn's sadness?
shrines and temples here
are all painted red

the large temple bell
struck by an American
has something
strange and funny in its ring
yet what prodigious sound!

36   MORI ŌGAI

[1] Nara, the capital of Japan from 710 to 784 A.D., is famous for its old temples, and attracts a great many tourists.

*Narabito wa aki no sabishisa miseji to ya yashiro mo tera mo ninuri
ni wa seshi*

ōgane wo Yankii tsukeri sono oto wa okashikeredomo ōkinaru oto

Yosano Akiko

The number of tanka Yosano Akiko wrote during her lifetime is estimated to be more than 40,000. She also published one novel, four volumes of stories for children, some 700 poems in free verse, and eighteen collections of essays on poetry, literature, and contemporary social issues. She also translated a number of Japanese classics into modern Japanese, including the massive *Genji monogatari* (The Tale of Genji). Her passion for promoting liberal education led her to help found Bunka Gakuin, a combination private girls' school and coeducational college. She did all that while raising eleven children.

Akiko, whose maiden name was Hō Shō, was born on December 7, 1878, to a merchant's family in the old city of Sakai near Osaka. Although her formal education went no farther than middle school, she loved books and read many Japanese classics while tending the family cake shop. She began writing tanka around 1894 and joined a local group of poets a couple of years later. The magazine *Myōjō*, edited by Yosano Tekkan, first accepted her tanka in May 1900. Her fateful meeting with Tekkan took place in August of that year, when he came to Osaka to lecture. They fell in love almost immediately, though Tekkan had a wife and child at the time. Akiko, knowing that there was no way her parents would bless such a union, left home in June of the following year and began to live at Tekkan's house in Tokyo. They were married that autumn, after Tekkan and his wife had reached a divorce agreement.

That was the beginning of Akiko's busy and productive life with Tekkan. A sociable woman, she often held verse-writing parties at home and invited poets to stay there for days. Fond of travel, she journeyed far to write poetry or to give lectures. In 1912 she joined her husband in Europe and met Auguste Rodin, Henri de Régnier, and Émile Verhaeren. In 1928 she and Tekkan traveled to China and Mongolia. As she grew older, her essays and lectures bacame more focused on social issues, especially on the need for improving the status of women. The sudden death of her husband in 1935 dealt her a severe blow but, thanks to her children and grandchildren, her life as a widow was not a lonely one. Her children also cared for her after she suffered a stroke in 1940. She died on May 29, 1942.

grabbing one of
my numerous poetic curses
scrawled and thrown away
I hold down
a black butterfly

into a pair of stars
we will turn—till then
let us never recall
autumn's voice
we heard in the same bed

noroiuta kaki kasanetaru hogo torite kuroki kochō wo osaenuru kana

*hoshi to narite awamu sore made omoi idena hitotsu fusuma ni kikishi
aki no koe*

a clear spring
inside me overflowed
and grew muddy
you are a child of sin
and so am I

pressing my breasts
with both hands
I kick open the door
to mystery
a flower in dark red

*mune no shimizu afurete tsuini nigorikeri kimi mo tsumi no ko ware
mo tsumi no ko*

*chibusa osae shinpi no tobari soto kerinu koko naru hana no kurenai
zo koki*

two chilly
spring days spent with you
on a Kyoto hill
unbefitting the plum blossoms
my hair in a tangle

camellias
and plum trees too
flower in white
only the peach blossoms
are not reproachful of my sin

*harusamu no futahi wo Kyō no yamagomori ume ni fusawanu waga
kami no midare*

*tsubaki sore mo ume mo sa nariki shirokariki waga tsumi towanu iro
momo ni miru*

young fingers
dissolving the white color
hesitate a moment
cold in the evening twilight
a magnolia blossom

writes poetry
that hand of hers
now stealing grapes
her hair soft and fine
rainbow at dawn

wakaki oyubi gofun wo toku ni madoi ari yūgure samuki mokuren no hana

uta no te ni budō wo nusumu ko no kami no yawarakaki kana niji no asaake

each shaped
like a small golden bird
ginko leaves
in the evening sunlight
flit down a hill

a white tower
unable to watch the battle
closes its eyes
in the rays of the evening sun
falling on dying soldiers[1]

YOSANO AKIKO   43

[1] Written during the Russo-Japanese War.

konjiki no chiisaki tori no katachi shite ichō chirunari yūhi no oka ni

tatakai wa miji to me tozuru hakutō ni nishibi shigurenu hito shinu yūbe

the peony in her hair
flared up, setting the ocean
on fire
the dream of a woman
whose thoughts are in a frenzy

tell them
she is enjoying the view
of the moon
a pink gossamer robe
barely covering her body

kazashitaru botan hi to nari umi moenu omoi midaruru hito no ko no yume

hanshin ni usukurenai no usumono no koromo matoite tsuki miru to ie

the earth looks
like one magnificent
lotus flower
as the sun rises
over the snowscape

warring heaven
has let fiery arrows fall
and cover the earth
with its scent
a field of poppies

chi wa hitotsu daibyakuren no hana to minu yuki no naka yori hi no
noboru toki

hisakata no ame no ikusa no hiya ochite nioi surunari keshi no
hanahara

the sea inside my heart
unknown even to myself
has a rock under its surface
and wrecks any approaching ship
no matter how much I cry

agonizing beyond words
this ailment
this hatred I feel
toward a pure maiden
totally unlike myself

46   YOSANO AKIKO

mune no umi ware dani shiranu anshō ni yabururu fune wa naku to iedomo

ii shiranu wazurai sunari ware ni ninu kiyoki otome wo nikumu yamai ni

but for women
writhing like vengeful demons
screaming like wild boars
no child of man
would ever be born[2]

the aster
has flowered
its pale purple
like the color of smoke
rising from my reverie

[2] One of the poems Akiko wrote after giving birth to her fourth daughter, a twin, with much difficulty. The other twin was stillborn.

akuryō to narite kurushimi i to narite nakazuwa hito no umigataki kana

shion saku waga kokoro yori noboritaru kemuri no gotoki usuiro wo shite

white blossoms bloom
on a thousand branches
in my grieving heart
despite the world outside
laden with fresh greens and reds[3]

evanescent
like the faint white
of cherry blossoms
blooming among the trees
my life on this spring day

[3] Written in the spring of 1935, shortly after the poet's husband died.

*kokoro naru kanashimi no hana chie shiroshi yo wa asamidori kurenai
ni shite*

*ko no ma naru someiyoshino no shiro hodo no hakanaki inochi idaku
haru kana*

Ishikawa Takuboku

Ishikawa Takuboku kept diaries intermittently from 1902 until his death in 1912. When he knew he was dying he asked his wife to burn all of them, but she did not do so. A year later she herself died. As Takuboku's posthumous fame rose, there grew an intense public demand to have the diaries made accessible, and after heated debates they were finally published in 1954. The extraordinary interest in the diaries was due in large part to the close connection Takuboku's poetry has with his actual life. Many of his tanka come alive only when read against the background of his biography. He was well aware of the connection and even used it to explain the reason for his writing tanka. "Poetry must be an honest diary," he said. "Hence, it must be fragmentary—it must not have unity."

Takuboku was born on February 20, 1886, the oldest son of a Zen priest who had his parish in the northeastern prefecture of Iwate. His childhood name was Kudō Hajime. He was an honors student in the early grades, but as he grew older he neglected his schoolwork to pursue his two passions: writing verses and his sweetheart's attention. He had to leave middle school without graduating, apparently because he cheated on examinations. That left him to pursue his two passions even more fervently, with happy results at first. At age sixteen he had a tanka accepted by *Myōjō* and subsequently had a number of poems published in other well-known magazines. At age nineteen he was able to marry his longtime girlfriend. In 1904, however, a turbulent period of his life began.

Takuboku's father was banished from his parish for not paying the proper fees to the headquarters of his sect. Trying to help family finances, young Takuboku took on miscellaneous jobs in rapid succession, moving from Iwate to Hokkaido to Tokyo, often leaving his family behind. No job lasted very long because his intense personality always created confrontations with his colleagues. Writing poetry was his only consolation, but it brought little income. He tried his hand at prose fiction, with worse results. Impoverished, he gradually came to blame society and developed an interest in socialism. In 1911 he and his friend Toki Zenmaro planned to found a left-wing magazine, but it did not materialize because he fell ill. The remainder of his life was wretched, hampered by illness, poverty, marital problems, feuds with friends and relatives, his father's disappearance, and his mother's death. The misery ended, at least for him, when he died of tuberculosis on April 13, 1912. He had written two volumes of tanka, *Ichiaku no suna* (A Handful of Sand) published in 1910, and *Kanashiki gangu* (Sad Toys), which appeared two months after his death.

just for fun
I put Mother on my back

she weighs so
little that I start crying

and can't walk three steps

young maidens
who hear me wailing thus

would say

it sounds like an ailing dog
howling at the moon

tawamure ni haha wo seoite / sono amari karoki ni nakite / sanpo ayumazu

waga naku wo otomera kikaba / yamainu no / tsuki ni hoyuru ni nitari to iuramu

words from
my dumbfounded mother

make me realize

I've been tapping a bowl
with my chopsticks[1]

mirror in hand

I make every kind
of face
that comes to mind

when I'm tired of crying

ISHIKAWA TAKUBOKU

[1] Japanese parents used to tell their children, as a way of teaching them not to play during a meal, that the sound of tapping a rice bowl with chopsticks tempts hungry demons to come out of hell.

akiretaru haha no kotoba ni / ki ga tsukeba / chawan wo hashi mote tatakite ariki

kagami tori / atau kagiri no samazama no kao wo shite minu / nakiakishi toki

on the roadside
a dog gives out a long
long yawn

I do the same

out of sheer envy

beastly face
with a mouth that opens
and closes

is all I see

of the man giving a talk

*michibata ni inu naganaga to akubi shinu / ware mo mane shimu /
urayamashisa ni*

*kemono meku kao ari kuchi wo aketate su / to nomi miteiru / hito no
kataru wo*

I work

and work yet my life
remains
impoverished as ever

I gaze at my hands

somehow

there looms a precipice
in my head

from where earth breaks loose
and comes falling down day by day

hatarakedo / hatarakedo nao waga kurashi raku ni narazari / jitto te
wo miru

nani ga nashi ni / atama no naka ni gake arite / higoto ni tsuchi no
kuzururu gotoshi

like a white lotus
blooming in a swamp

sorrow

beautifully clear
floats in my befuddled mind

as if in water

my body is submerged
in sorrow

that smells a little
of green onions this evening

shiroki hasu numa ni saku gotoku / kanashimi ga / ei no aida ni hakkiri to uku

mizu no goto / karada wo hitasu kanashimi ni / negi no ka nado no majireru yūbe

when I breathe

there is something that moans
in my chest

a moan lonelier
than the autumn wind!

I close my eyes

yet nothing whatever
floats up in my mind

out of sheer loneliness
I reopen them

*iki sureba, / mune no uchi nite naru oto ari. / kogarashi yori mo
sabishiki sono oto!*

*me tozuredo / kokoro ni ukabu nani mo nashi. / sabishiku mo mata
me wo akeru kana.*

accidentally
having broken a teacup

I learned the joy
of breaking something

it's on my mind this morning too

sorrow
its outlines blurred

at nightfall

sneaks into the room
and sits on my bed

ayamachite chawan wo kowashi, / mono wo kowasu kimochi no yosa wo, / kesa mo omoeru.

bon'yari to shita kanashimi ga, / yo to nareba, / nedai no ue ni sotto kite noru.

fearing
what lies in my heart
may be heard

I quickly draw back my chest

from the stethoscope

the color
of fresh vegetable salad

is so pleasing

I pick up the chopsticks
and yet. . . and yet. . .

*omou koto nusumi kikaruru gotoku nite, / tsuto mune wo hikinu— /
chōshinki yori.*

*atarashiki sarado no iro no /   ureshisa ni, / hashi toriagete mi wa
mitsuredomo—*

has Fate sneaked in
and mounted on my body?

so I wonder

waking in the middle of night
under the weight of the quilt

sadly

something in my heart
does not wish
my illness to be cured

I peer into my heart

*unmei no kite noreru ka to / utagainu— / futon no omoki yowa no
nezame ni.*

*kanashiku mo / yamai iyuru wo negawazaru kokoro ware ni ari. /
nan no kokoro zo.*

what always seemed
a little remote from me

the forlorn
anguish of a terrorist

   draws close to me of late

           forgetting
           my illness for a moment

           I try
           to bellow like an ox—

               before my wife and child come home

*yaya tōki mono ni omoishi / terorisuto no kanashiki kokoro mo— /
chikazuku hi no ari.*

*aruhi, futo, yamai wo wasure, / ushi no naku mane wo shite minu,— /
tsuma ko no rusu ni.*

Saitō Mokichi

Like Mori Ōgai, Saitō Moki-
chi was educated as a scientist and subsequently had a
successful medical career. However, whereas Ōgai was a
man of penetrating intellect who would analyze a subject
down to the last detail, Mokichi had a more spiritual
respect for nature and was more inclined to leave its
mysteries unplumbed. As a result, his poetry is less acces-
sible than Ōgai's. Obviously that was largely due to his
temperament, but it might also have had something to
do with the rugged scenery of northeastern Japan, where
he spent his childhood.

Mokichi was born on May 14, 1882, at a small village
in Yamagata prefecture. His father, surnamed Moriya,
was a farmer. Mokichi might have become a farmer, too,
if it had not been for his outstanding academic record in
primary school. A relative of his family, a physician
named Saitō Kiichi, wanted him to get a higher educa-
tion and invited him to come and live at his home in
Tokyo. Thus Mokichi moved to Tokyo at age fourteen
and prepared himself for a medical career. In 1905 he
officially became a member of the Saitō family by mar-
rying one of Kiichi's daughters. It was around this time
that he read Shiki's tanka and began writing seriously in
that verse form. In 1908 he became a founding member
of the magazine *Araragi* and three years later joined its
editorial board. His first book of tanka, entitled *Shakkō*
(Red Lights) and published in 1913, immediately estab-
lished his reputation. From 1917 on, however, he had to
devote more time to his medical career, as he moved to

Nagasaki to serve on the faculty of a local college. In 1921 he traveled to Germany to study psychiatry and stayed in Europe for the next three years. Upon returning to Tokyo he resumed his double career with renewed vigor, becoming the editor-publisher of *Araragi* in 1926 and succeeding his father-in-law as director of Aoyama Mental Hospital the following year. As he grew older, he developed a scholarly interest in *Man'yōshū*, especially in the poetry of the earliest major poet included in it. His massive book on Kakinomoto Hitomaro won him a Japan Academy Award in 1940. During the war years he wrote a number of nationalistic poems, but the war he supported victimized him in the end, for both his home and his hospital were burnt to the ground in air raids in 1945. Already in his sixties, he had to spend the next three years at rented quarters in his native village. Though some critics attacked him for his wartime poems, he received a number of honors in his last years, including a Yomiuri Literature Prize in 1950 and an Order of Cultural Merit the following year. He died of a heart ailment on February 25, 1953. His complete works, published between 1952 and 1957, consist of fifty-six volumes, testifying to the inexhaustible energy he displayed throughout his long career.

from where
a red tomato
lies rotting
I am only
a few steps away

the yolk
of a chicken egg
crumbling out of shape
this wretchedness I feel
during the long seasonal rain

akanasu no kusarete itaru tokoro yori ikuhodo mo naki ayumi narikeri

*niwatori no tamago no kimi no midare yuku samidare goro no
ajikinaki kana*

red pepper pods
all over the farm
next to a lane
where stands a youngster
with small eyes

a self-portrait
of Gauguin
makes me recall the day
when I killed wild silkworms
in the mountains of the north

ichimen ni tōgarashi akaki hatamichi ni tateru warabe no manako chiisashi

Googan no jigazō mireba michinoku ni yamako koroshishi sono hi omooyu

ever so close
to the colors of life on earth
this keeper of madmen
with tears of blood
welling up in his eyes

snowflakes
falling from the misted sky
make me feel the heart
of an imprisoned criminal
gulping down a meal

yo no iro no katawara ni ite kyōjamori ki naru namida wa waki idenikeri

ama kirashi yuki furu mireba ii wo kū shūjin no kokoro ware ni wakitari

past the hens
bathing in the dirt
soundlessly
a razor sharpener
walks and is gone

nothing to be done?
on the palm of my hand
that has killed a firefly
lies its light so utterly crushed
nothing at all to be done

66   SAITŌ MOKICHI

mendorira suna abi itare hissori to kamisoritogi wa sugi yukinikeri

sube naki ka hotaru wo korosu tenohira ni hikari tsuburete sen sube
wa nashi

dahlias are black
a laughing madman said
and walked away
not looking back
even once

a fly
cutting across the darkness
with all its strength
crashes into the shoji screen
a faint sound

daariya wa kuroshi waraite sari yukeru kyōjin wa tsuini kaerimizukeri

hitaburuni ankoku wo tobu hae hitotsu shōji ni ataru oto zo kikoyuru

from the evening darkness
of the low sky
unreached by the lamplight
a moth
came flying in

aspiration
for the stillness
of death?
clouds trailing across the sky
above the Indian Ocean[1]

[1] Written in 1924, during a trip back from Europe.

dentō no hikari todokanu yoiyami no hikuki sora yori ga wa tobite kitsu

inochi shinishi nochi no shizukesa wo negawamu ka Indo no umi ni tanabikeru kumo

often likened
to a maiden's nipples
the grapes
piled in a heap
so very close to me

confinement
with black curtains
hanging down to the floor
this one hour and a half
is also part of my life[2]

[2] Written in 1944, after Allied air attacks on Tokyo began. Residents were required to
remain indoors while air-raid warnings were in force. At night all windows had to be
covered with black curtains.

*maotome no chibusa no gotoshi to iwaretaru budō wo tsuminu waga
majikaku ni*

*anmaku wo hikuku oroshite komoritaru ichijikan-han mo waga yo to
zo omou*

what on the other shore
tugs at its heart so?
in the evening dusk
over the Mogami River
a lone firefly

determined to try
living as an old man
in the new age
like a chestnut
fallen on the forest floor[3]

[3] Written in 1947, the year Japan's new constitution went into effect.

*kano kishi ni nani wo motomuru yoiyami no Mogamigawa no ue no
hitotsu hotaru wa*

*atarashiki tokiyo ni oite ikimu to su yama ni ochitaru kuri no gotoku
ni*

by the road
a castor oil plant
flowering
something like a profound
feeling of guilt[4]

frog
just out of its hole
swallowing
the sunlight of spring
reflected on the snow

SAITŌ MOKICHI   71

[4] Also written in 1947. Castor oil plants were grown in Japan during the war for the
purpose of producing lubricant for military planes.

*michi no be ni hima no hana sakitarishi koto nani ka tsumi fukaki
kanji no gotoku*

*ana ideshi kaeru ga yuki ni hansha suru haru no hikari wo
nomitsutsu itari*

all that past life
I have lived
not unlike
a fallen cedar leaf
in the dusky woods

infinitely far
beyond this heaven and earth
where
empty space comes to an end
a sound of the blowing wind

waga ikishi katsute no sei mo kuragari no sugi no ochiba to
omowazarame ya

ametsuchi no sokie no kiwami tōdōshi munashiki hate ni kaze no fuku
oto

Kitahara Hakushū

According to a chronology of his life published in 1917, at age three Kitahara Hakushū "despaired of life and attempted suicide"; he "took up smoking and roamed the street with a cigarette in his mouth" at age four. It seems that an aura of mystery began to shroud Hakushū's biography when he was still a young man. He himself did not mind a mystique growing around him; indeed, there is evidence that at times he bent over backward to give credence to the mystique.

Kitahara Ryūkichi, later Hakushū, was born in northern Kyushu on January 25, 1885. His father was the owner of a sake brewery in Yanagawa, but his business never recovered after the brewery burned down in 1901. Hakushū became interested in writing verses in middle school and entered the English Department of Waseda University in 1904. In Tokyo his brilliant poetic talent immediately attracted the attention and friendship of leading tanka poets such as the Yosanos, Takuboku, and Mokichi. But his national debut as a poet was with two free-verse collections published in 1909 and 1911. It was in 1913 that his first book of tanka, entitled *Kiri no hana* (Paulownia Flowers), appeared and received high critical acclaim. Unfortunately these books produced little income, and his personal life became even more strained when a lawsuit was brought against him by a neighbor whose wife he had fallen in love with. After settling the suit out of court, Hakushū married the woman and moved away from Tokyo, but the marriage lasted for less than two years. He married another woman in 1916 and divorced her four years later. Around this time he turned to writing songs and stories for children, which helped to stabilize his life financially. His third wife, whom he married in 1921, also provided a more peaceful home for him. A son was born in 1922 and a daughter in 1925, and he was often seen traveling with his family. His literary production also increased, so much so that his collected works, published from 1929 to 1934, totaled eighteen volumes. Many years of hard work, however, had been slowly undermining his health. In 1937 he began to have eye hemorrhages, and gradually lost his eyesight. Yet he still continued traveling and writing poetry. Some scholars think his greatest poetic achievement came with *Kurohi* (The Black Cypress), a collection of tanka written in this phase of his life. He died on November 2, 1942, after saying, "This is my new start."

spring bird
do not sing, please do not
as this day ends
the blazing red sun
is falling on the grassy field

the strong scent
of a wilting flower
clings to my body
above the squalid alley
a spring night's moon

.

*haru no tori na nakiso nakiso akaaka to to no mo no kusa ni hi no iru
yūbe*

*shiore yuku takaki hana no ka mi ni shimitsu mazushiki machi no
haru no yo no tsuki*

in my heart
something resembling a canal
at twilight
a dream soft and fragile
drifting alone on the stream

today too
out of this urge to cry
I went to the city
and out of this urge to cry
came home from the city

*tasogare no suiro ni nitaru kokoro ari yawarakaki yume no hitori
nagaruru*

*kyō mo mata nakamahoshisa ni machi ni ide nakamahoshisa ni
machi yori kaeru*

I sneaked into
an abandoned garden
and stepped on
a dandelion's whiteness
spring past its prime

an ailing child
plays a harmonica
into the night
above the cornfield
a yellow moon in ascent

sutaretaru sono ni fumi iri tanpopo no shiroki wo fumeba haru takenikeru

yameru ko wa hamonika wo fuki yo ni irinu morokoshibata no ki naru tsuki no de

almost invisible
on the tip of my finger
a blue scar
painfully absorbing
the glare of summer

my uncle
nursing a stroke
in his country house
gazes at a red flower
this spring evening

yubisaki no aru ka naki ka no aoki kizu sore ni mo natsu wa shimite hikarinu

inakaya ni chūbūyami no waga oji ga akaki hana miru haru no yūgure

each alighted
on a thick onion leaf
dragonflies
look fearful of something
in the crimson sunset glow

after lunch
this lonely feeling
as the spring day
begins to settle
the color of black tea

futonegi no hitokuki goto ni tonbo ite nani ka osoruru akaki yūgure

hirugedoki hateshi sabishisa haru no hi mo kōcha no iro ni shizumi sometsutsu

At a hospital in Tokyo
during the summer
of 1911

summer's loneliness
as the anesthetic slowly
numbs my mind
the singing of an insect
sounding like a bell

gleaming sliver
of the third-day moon
above the cornfield
where cornstalks stand awake
as cornstalks always do

*natsu wa sabishi kororohorumu ni shibire yuku waga kokoro ni mo
nakeru suzumushi*

*mika no tsuki hosoku kirameku kibibatake kibi wa kibi to shi me no
samete itsu*

in the daytime
its faint light flickering
a firefly
from a grove of giant bamboos
no sooner comes out than is gone

after letting my wife
leave me because of our poverty
I put together
a trellis for my morning glory
with bamboos and a rope

*hiru nagara kasukani hikaru hotaru hitotsu mōsō no yabu wo idete
kietari*

*mazushisa ni tsuma wo kaeshite asagao no kakine yuiori take to nawa
mote*

magnolia
blossoming in white clusters
at daybreak
the eastern sky resounds
with the roar of thunder

autumn bellflower
with only one bloom as yet
near a sparrow
hopping with bare feet
that look cool and light

hoo no hana shiroku muragaru yoakegata himugashi no sora ni rai wa todoroku

kichikō wa hitohana nagara waki ariku suzume no suashi suzushiku karoshi

almost invisible
on the flowing water
a blue bubble
touched by the tail feathers
of a wagtail

winter day
on a chilly plate
lies a pheasant
its eyes looking white
with the eyelids closed

*yuku mizu no me ni todomaranu aominawa sekirei no o wa fure ni
tarikeri*

*fuyu hiyaki sara no ue ni wa yamadori no manabuta shiroshi tojishi
manabuta*

gasoline
coal tar, a smell of lumber
a blooming daphne
various scents of deepening spring
as I walk this dark night

during a fit
of hectic coughing
that almost strangles the throat
a strange calm
for a fraction of a second

gasorin kōrutā kiga jinchō to kanji kite haru shigeshi mo yo yamiyo
yukunari

hito sekite iki tsukimu toki kasukekari funbyō no nagi nashi to
iwanakuni

Shaku Chōkū

Apparently Shaku Chōkū wanted to think of himself as two persons pursuing two different careers. While he published poetry and fiction under that name, he used his real name, Orikuchi Shinobu, when he wrote scholarly essays in literature and ethnology. Inevitably, the two careers came in contact with each other, and the contact was by no means harmful to either career. His scholarly research on the origins of Japanese culture benefited from his fertile poetic imagination, while his tanka was enriched by his extensive knowledge of the way people lived in ancient times.

Chōkū was born in Osaka on February 11, 1887. His father operated a drugstore, but since childhood Chōkū seems to have been keenly conscious of his great-grandfather, a Shinto priest. When he reached college age he decided to continue his education at Kokugakuin University, which was known for its Shinto studies. His interest in Shintoism led him to do research in ancient Japanese culture, which prompted him to travel to remote areas of Japan in search of myths, legends, and folk tales. In the same spirit he studied *Man'yōshū* extensively, publishing a modern translation of it in 1917 and a dictionary in 1919. He started teaching at Kokugakuin University the same year, and at Keio University in 1923. Never married, he enjoyed associating with students and often took them on his research trips. He became especially close to one of them and eventually made him his adopted son, but before the official procedure was completed the young man was drafted by the army and sent to Iwo Jima, where he was killed in 1945. The death caused Chōkū profound grief and permanently clouded his later years, despite the high honors awarded him by various organizations during the postwar period. A book of poetry he published in 1948 was awarded an Academy of Arts Prize. He was elected to the Japan Science Council the same year. In 1949 he was appointed as a judge in the New Year's Tanka Contest sponsored by the Imperial Household. A thirty-two-volume set of his complete works won him the Emperor's Prize, but he did not live to receive the award. He died of cancer on September 3, 1954. The Shaku Chōkū Prize, established in his memory, is now one of the highest honors a tanka poet can receive.

which child
is flying that kite?

the year's last day

in the vast empty sky
a flapping sound

New Year's temple bells
have stopped ringing

in the silent world
nothing but

my agitated voice

*dono ko no aguramu tako zo.   ōmisoka   munashiki sora no tadanaka
ni naru*

*joya no kane tsuki osametari.   shizukanaru seken ni hitori   waga
ikaru koe*

after enduring
an endless day

of silence

this midnight hour
I mutter all alone

the train speeds on

clear in the darkness of night
the glimmering frost

in this cold
no human life will expire[1]

[1] Written late in 1917, when the poet's mother was stricken by illness and he rushed to her
bedside. She died in February of the following year.

*nagaki hi no moda no hisashiki tae kitsutsu, kono sayonaka ni
hitori mono iu*

*kisha hashiru yamiyo ni shiruki shimo no teri. kono sayakesani, hito
wa shinaji mo*

a phantom appears

colors of waves
at a turbulent channel

I spend the New Year's Eve
seated on the tatami floor

from the water's depth
my face in the present world
looks up at me

what loneliness awaits me
in the world to come?

*keshiki tatsu.   hayasui no to no nami no iro.   toshi no yo wo suwaru
tatami no ue ni*

*minasoko ni, utsusomi no omowa shizuki miyu.   komu yo mo, ware no
sabishiku aramu*

nowhere on the leaves
a sign of deep slumber
and yet, from the silk tree

a drifting scent allures me
to love my life on this earth

arrowroot flowers
lie trampled on the ground
their colors fresh

someone has climbed ahead of me
along this mountain path

nemu no ha no fukaki nemuri wa mienedomo, utsusomi oshiki sono
kaori tachi

kuzu no hana fumi shidakarete, iro atarashi. kono yamamichi wo
yukishi hito ari

late at night in the kitchen
lit by the fire
I boil chicken, roast fish
and enjoy myself all alone

Imamiya Middle School

how to follow
the ways of the world
is not what I taught

many blunders made by
so many of those I taught[2]

[2] The poet taught at Imamiya Middle School in Osaka for three years, beginning in 1911.
The poem was written some fifteen years later.

*kuriyabe no yofuke / akaaka hi wo tsukete, / tori wo ni uo wo yaki, /
hitori tanoshiki*

*yo no naka ni shitagau michi wo / tokazariki. / ayamachi ōki /
oshiego no kazu*

town children
playing with swords

    see how utterly
    our age has become
    weary of peace

        imagining
        the grassy ground not shown
        in the newsreel
        of a victorious battle

        I grieve

*machi no ko no tachi furi asobi / miru sae ni, / yo wa shizukesa ni, /
uminikerashi mo*

*isamashiki niusu eiga ni, utsuri konu kusamura-zuchi wo omoi
kanashimu*

somewhere around
Lord Buddha's eyes

I keep seeing
the sadness of a weary man

as I trudge along this road

Vultures
—in the midst of war

flocking together
crying and swooping down

vultures in the sky

underneath
I keep walking

*mihotoke no bimoku no hodo no   unjitaru sabishisa wo omou.   kono
michi no aida*

*muragarite   nakitsutsu kudaru   ōzora no shichō no shita wo   ware wa
yukunari*

my research
aiming to uncover and tell

how beautiful
love was in the distant past

draws close to an end

                                        kidnapping
                                        armed robbery
                                        burglary

                                        committed by people
                                        other than me

                                        the news boggles my mind[3]

[3] Written during the chaotic postwar period.

*tōtsu yo no koi no aware wo   tsutae koshi waga gakumon mo,   owari
chikazuku*

*hitokadoi   hihagi   nusubito   ware naranu hito no suru mite   kokoro
odoroku*

a bulky oil lamp
I have carried out
fills my heart with joy

like ancient learning
it sits there, silent

oddly shaped
a doll

from time to time
seems to come dancing

out of my mind

ōkinaru ranpu tōdete yorokoberi. furuki chishiki no gotoku shizukeki

*kimyōnaru ningyō hitotsu   tokidoki ni odori deru gotoshi. waga
kokoro yori*

among the hundreds
of tubercular patients

I see one
all gaunt with age

my former love

on Christmas Eve

voices of myriad demons
marching this way

at least I see a cat
sucking at my calf

*ikuhyaku no shiwabukiyami no naka ni miru   oi saraboeru   furuki
koibito*

*yaso tanjōe no yoi ni   kozori kuru mono no koe.   sukunakumo neko
wa waga kobura suu*

Toki Zenmaro

Journalists are expected to show curiosity about all human activities, but few in Japan have pursued the objects of their curiosity as extensively as Toki Zenmaro. Despite his busy career as a newspaper reporter, Zenmaro authored many scholarly books on classical Japanese literature, one of them winning a Japan Academy Award. He also wrote a number of new noh plays and had them performed by professional actors. He translated the great Chinese poet Tu Fu (712-770) so extensively as to fill four volumes. Nevertheless, unlike most classical scholars, he advocated writing Japanese in the Roman alphabet and brought out a romanized edition of *Man'yōshū*. He was also a leader of the Japan Esperanto Society. An avid sports fan, he invented a game called *ekiden*, a long-distance relay race, which is still popular in Japan. And, of course, he was a poet who published more than thirty books of tanka during his lifetime.

Born in Tokyo on June 8, 1885, Zenmaro learned the pleasure of writing tanka from his father, a Buddhist priest and amateur poet, when he was still a small child. His inquisitive mind always found plenty of topics, especially after he graduated from Waseda University and began working for Yomiuri Press in 1908. His first volume of tanka, published in 1910 and entitled *Nakiwarai* (Tearful Smile), shocked readers because all the poems were in Roman letters. Another bold venture came three years later, when he founded *Seikatsu to geijutsu*, a magazine that accommodated left-wing writers and activists. In 1918 he moved to Asahi Press and continued to work there until reaching the retirement age in 1940. His life was even more busy after retirement, as he was asked to serve as executive of a publishing house, head of a public library, college professor, chair of the National Council on the Japanese Language, and many other positions. Although his house was destroyed by fire twice, first in the Great Tokyo Earthquake of 1923, and again in an air raid during World War II, he always seemed to overcome personal disaster by engaging himself in new ventures. Even at age ninety, he was seen traveling to China on a public mission. He died in Tokyo on April 15, 1980. His last words were: "I have lived fully. I am grateful."

How sad it is
to be a worker with
white hands!
　　I read a censored book,
　　tears streaming down my cheeks.

It's hazardous
to live in Japan and say
in the language
of the Japanese people
　　what's on my mind.

TOKI ZENMARO　　99

*te no shiroki rōdōsha koso kanashikere. /　kokkin no sho wo, /　namida
shite yomeri.*

*Nippon ni sumi, / Nippon no kuni no kotoba mote iu wa ayaushi, /
waga omou koto.*

"We're poor
because we don't work."

"We'll be poor
even if we do."

"We'll work anyway."

Tears, tears,

streaming from the tired brain
to the eyes,

clearly
showing their paths.

*"hatarakanu yue mazushiki naramu." / "hatarakite mo mazushikaru
beshi." / "tomokaku mo hatarakamu."*

*namida, namida, / tsukareshi nō yori mabuta e, / nagaruru michi no
hakkiri to miyu.*

In sullen silence
he works.
           In sullen silence
           I walk
           toward him.

All the young men I know
are penniless.
     This man, and that man too.
All the young men I know
are penniless.
     Winter.

muttsuri to kare wa hataraku, / muttsuri to / sono katawara ni,
ware, chikazukinikeri.

waga shireru seinen wa mina mazushi, / kare mo, kare mo / waga
shireru seinen wa mina mazushi, fuyu.

On the birth of my son

Don't be like
your cowardly
father.
    Never take after
    his compromising nature.

On the road
I've picked up stones.
Too furious
I don't know
what to throw them at.

nare no chichi no / kono okubyō ni niru nakare, / kono akirame wo manuru koto nakare.

michi no ue ni ishi wa hiroitsu, kuruoshiku nani ni mukaite nagubeki wo shirazu.

September 1, 1923

danger!
get out this moment!
calling out
I peer into the darkness
no sign of life anywhere[1]

At the lectern

when I say something
to make them laugh
they laugh
living at a time
that can't be passed in laughter

TOKI ZENMARO   103

---

[1] Written on the day of the Great Tokyo Earthquake. Zenmaro's house was completely destroyed in a fire that swept the neighborhood.

ayaushi ima wa nogarene to koe kakete mayami wo nozoku sudeni kage nashi

warawasureba warau nari waraite wa kesshite sumasarezaru jidai naru ni

Nothing
but reason
can be depended on.
That reason
is dipped in a flowing
stream of tears.

New York

I walk among men
who look as though they might
sneak up to me
and without a word
stick a gun in my armpit

*tayoru mono wa risei no hoka ni nai, sono risei wo nagareru ga mama
no namida ni hitasu*

*sotto yorisotte waki no shita e mugon no pisutoru wo sashimukesōna
otoko no aida wo tōru*

having lived
from the start
in a depressing age
I don't feel it—
says a man
younger than I

an old soldier
lodged in our house
tells a war story
that says nothing
about killing an enemy

TOKI ZENMARO   105

hajime yori yūutsunaru jidai ni ikitarishikaba shika mo kanzezu to iu
hito no ware yori mo wakaki

waga ie wo shukusha to shitsuru rōhei no ikusagatari wa teki wo
korosazu

Evidence

abandoned corpses
hundreds in one report
thousands in another
there is no person
blessed with two lives[2]

old Japan
self-destroyed and dying
before my eyes
a testimony to the worth
of what I have lived by[3]

[2] Written in 1940, during the undeclared war with China.
[3] Written in 1945, after the end of World War II.

iki shitai sūhyaku to ii sūsen to iu inochi wo futatsu mochishi mono nashi

furuki Nippon no jikai jimetsu shi yuku sugata wo me no mae ni shite ikeru shirushi ari

no news of him
after he led a troop
into the mountains
flowers of the morning glory
beginning to fade[4]

work on the impossible
and change it into the possible
preached our past militarist leaders
our government today
works on the possible
and changes it into the impossible[5]

[4] Written on August 15, 1946, exactly one year after the end of the war. Zenmaro's son-in-law was among the numerous Japanese soldiers still missing in the war.
[5] Published in 1947. Consisting of forty-one Japanese syllables, the poem is among the longest free-style tanka written by Zenmaro.

hei wo hikiite yama ni irishi nochi no shōsoku nashi asagao no hana wa saki sugimu to su

fukanō wo kanō to seyo to iishi gunbatsu ariki ima wa kanō wo fukanō to suru seifu ari

At the Van Gogh exibition

the crazed life
of someone who reached truth
at the end
of a quest for beauty
is here with me

On *Mumonkan*[6]

where there is neither
a stone nor a bamboo

I wish to hear

the sound of a stone
hitting a bamboo

[6] *Mumonkan* (The Gateless Barrier) is a Zen classic written by the Chinese monk Hui K'ai during the Sung Dynasty. Zenmaro became increasingly interested in Buddhism and wrote several plays on Buddhist themes during his last years.

bi wo motomete shin ni itareru kyūkyoku no kurueru inochi ima koko ni ari

ishi mo take mo naki tokoro nite   kikan to su   take ni atarishi ishi no hibiki wo

Okamoto Kanoko

"A woman of beauty, nobility, and creative talent emerges only where there is a life of spiritual and material luxury." That is what the novelist Kawabata Yasunari said about Okamoto Kanoko. She was fortunate to have a number of understanding people around her, who enabled her to lead such a privileged existence. Still, her sensibility was too delicate, too tender, and too aware of itself to allow her peace of mind. She had periods of deep depression, for which she eventually sought help in religion. In that process, she made some outstanding contributions to literature.

Kanoko was born Ōnuki Kano in Tokyo on March 1, 1889. Because her father was a wealthy businessman, she was brought up in affluence, and was tutored in literature and the arts even before school age. She wrote her first tanka at age seven and had her poems first published in her early teens. When she was still in middle school, she met the Yosanos and had her tanka accepted by *Myōjō* in 1906. A precocious girl in other ways too, she had many boyfriends and eloped with one of them. In the end, however, she married a young artist, Okamoto Ippei, in 1910 and gave birth to three children in the next five years. Still far from settling into domesticity, she continued to see other young men and even persuaded her husband to let one of them live in their house. Tormented with guilt, she began to have nervous breakdowns. Intitially she sought help from Christianity, then turned to Mahayana Buddhism. Her extramarital romances, however, did not stop. In 1929 Kanoko, her husband, and their son started on a journey to Europe, taking two of her boyfriends with them. They spent eleven months in London, six months in Paris, and five months in Berlin. In 1936, with Kawabata's encouragement, Kanoko began to concentrate her creative energy on writing the prose fiction for which she is best known today. She wrote nine collections of fiction in the next three years, although only five of them were published before her death. She died of a stroke on February 18, 1939. She had published four books of tanka during her lifetime.

twenty days
of sojourn in the woods
and yet
not a single tree willing
to take me in its warm embrace

innately reserved
a silkworm does not cry
or sing out
but seals its grief-laden heart
in a cocoon it weaves

OKAMOTO KANOKO   111

*yama ni kite hatsuka henuredo atatakaku ware wo ba idaku ichiju
dani nashi*

*tsutsumashiku nakanu utawanu ko ga kokoro kanashiku komete mayu
amareken*

stark naked
I hold in my hand
a red apple
holding it in my hand
I take a morning bath

cherry blossoms
blooming with all the strength
they possess
oblige me to view them
with all the strength I possess

*hadaka nite ware wa mochitari kurenai no ringo mochitari asaburo no
naka ni*

*sakurabana inochi ippai ni saku karani inochi wo kakete waga
nagametari*

they don't appeal to me
those cherry blossoms
blooming today
as I am far too busy
counting the lies he has told

ten years ago
I was a madwoman
with eyes fixed on
fiery red cherry blossoms
inky black cherry blossoms

kyō sakeru sakura wa ware ni yō araji hito no uso wo ba hitani kazouru

kyōjin no ware ga minikeru totose mae no makkana sakura makuroki sakura

as I gaze upon
a bundle of small red roses
with fear in my heart
each and every flower
turns into an eye

                              a flower blooms
                              showing the natural color
                              it was born with
                              while I have never known
                              in what color I am to bloom

114   OKAMOTO KANOKO

osore moteru waga mite areba beni kobara hitotsu hitotsu mina me to
narinikeri

onozu kara naru inochi no iro ni hana sakeri waga saku iro wo ware
wa shiranu ni

if I were to stand
with roots in the ground
like a flower
would my life bloom out
in the color I was born with?

selfish woman
locking herself at home
gazes at a weed
stretching its vines selfishly
wherever it wishes to

*hana no gotoku tsuchi ni shi tataba waga inochi onozu kara naru iro
ni sakamu ka*

*wagamamana onna komorite wagamamani nobiyuku kusa no tsuru
wo mite ori*

a cockscomb
so excessively red
makes me wonder
if I am losing my senses
it's so excessively red

having let flow
all the blood to flow
in the kitchen
a dead fish lies gleaming
in the stillness of noon

keitō wa amarini akashi yo waga kuruu kizashi ni mo aru ka amarini
akashi yo

nagaruru chi nagashi tsukushite kuriyabe ni shigyo hikaru nari hiru
no shizukesa

to the sea, to the sea
single-mindedly I have come
yet nothing is here
except the sea stretching
into an infinite distance

I measure
the size of my head
not knowing
what else to do
with my own stubbornness

*umi e umi e to hitamukini kinu koko no umi nan ni mo arazute tada
harukekari*

*waga atama no ōkisa nado wo hakaritari waga gōjō wo moteamashi
tsutsu*

it stands
looking over the waves
far in the offing
a magnificent sunflower
blooming with all its might

where
a crabapple lets fall
its pink petals
some little larvae
crawl on the earth

*oki tsu nami no nami ni mukaite tairin no himawari tateri hirakikiri
tsutsu*

kaidō no hanabira akaku chiru tokoro chi ni yōchū wa hai itarikeri

my mind shattered
in thousands of fragments
wishes to spend
this whole day on a boat
drifting with the river stream

green leaves
so brightly green
red flowers
so brightly red
how pleasant to my eyes!

OKAMOTO KANOKO   119

*omoi koso chijinare ware wo kyō hitohi fune ni makasete kawa ni wa
ukame*

*aoki ha no ao azayakeshi akaki hana no aka azayakeshi mitsutsu
tanoshiki*

an insect
born too early in spring
had been given
such tender care in a cage
finally it died

cherry petals
each disintegrating
its flowery form
mingles with the small gravel
trampled by people who pass

haru hayaku umareshi mushi no osanaki wo ko ni itawarite
shinashimenikeri

sakurabana katai wo tokite hito no fumu komakaki zari ni majirikeru
kamo

Miyazawa Kenji

As a writer of free verse and juvenile fiction, Miyazawa Kenji is a towering figure in the history of modern Japanese literature. Yet it is doubtful that he wanted to be remembered as such. His occupational training was in agricultural chemistry, and during his short life he spent a great deal of time and energy advising farmers on fertilizing and soil conditioning. He was also a devout Buddhist and took an active role in propagating the Buddha's teachings. Though he wrote poetry—and outstanding poetry at that—he was far more than a poet, and the unique quality of his literary writings derives from that fact.

Kenji was born in a rural town in Iwate prefecture on August 27, 1896. Because his father operated a pawnshop, he witnessed the plight of local peasants from early childhood and gradually came to consider it his mission to help them. This sense of mission intensified as he became seriously interested in Buddhism during middle school. Against the wishes of his father, who wanted him to take over the family business, he entered Morioka College of Agriculture in 1915 and graduated from it three years later. From 1921 to 1926 he taught agriculture at a high school near his parents' home. The reason he resigned his teaching post was that he wanted to become a farmer. Subsequently he moved to a shack and began to cultivate a wild area around it. He also set up a social and educational club for local farmers, where he gave free lectures on farming as well as on poetry and music. Unfortunately his dedication led him to overwork. In

1928 he contracted pleurisy and then pneumonia, from which he never completely recovered. He died on September 21, 1933. He was seen giving advice to a farmer on fertilizing the day before his death.

Kenji's literary fame, which came posthumously, is largely based on his free verse and stories for children, such as those collected in *Haru to Shura* (Spring and Asura) and *Chūmon no ōi ryōriten* (The Restaurant of Many Orders). But his interest in creative writing started with tanka, probably because the middle school he attended happened to be Takuboku's alma mater. In any case, he began writing tanka in 1911, while he was a student at that school. During the next ten years he drafted over one thousand poems in the thirty-one-syllable form and published some of them in local magazines. He wrote very few tanka after 1920, as his creative energy turned toward writing free verse and juvenile literature. Interestingly, though, the last two poems he wrote were tanka.

like cracks
veining a porcelain vase
lean branches
partition the gloomy
white sky

bloodshot
the bow-shaped moon
in the depth of night
comes to my window
and curls its lips

*setomono no hibiware no gotoku hosoeda wa sabishiku shiroki sora wo
wakachinu*

*chibashireru yumihari no tsuki waga mado ni mayonaka kitarite
kuchi wo yugamuru*

red rag
of membrane
hangs in my throat
a bitter quarrel
with Father again

at last
the sky has been covered up
with toadskin
its yellow sheen
its poisonous sheen

*nenmaku no akaki borokire nodo ni burasagari chichi to kanashiki
isakai wo suru*

*sosa wa ima hiki no kawa nite hararetari sono ki no hikari sono doku
no hikari*

with red eyes
and numerous body joints
creatures gather
like floating weeds
and hop around in my brain

lightning
flashes again
in purple
letting my white lily bloom
to its heart's content

*me wa akaku kansetsu ōki dōbutsu ga mo no gotoku murete nō wo
hanearuku*

*inabikari mata murasaki ni hiramekeba waga shirayuri wa omoikiri
sakeri*

left alone
on the seashore washed by
oxygen waves
someone pounding hemp
like a machine

unsettled
sky in the twilight
mountains
breathing with life
surround the riverbed

yorube naki sanso no nami no kishi ni ite kikai no gotoku asa wo utsu hito

ochitsukanu tasogare no sora yamayama wa ikitaru gotoku kawara wo kakomu

scattered clouds

a beetle bites at the pistils
of a lily

its back mirroring
the sky above the valley

phosphorescence
in the eyes of a deer
fleeing back to its home
and the dark half
of the fifth-night moon

*chigiregumo / yuri no shibe kamu kōchū no / sena ni utsureru
yamakai no sora*

*nige kaeru shika no manako no rinkō to nakaba wa kuroki itsuka no
tsuki to*

steel pen
steel pen
you are the only one
roaming the wasteland
of my doubting mind

snow has fallen
making the evil cypress
of yesterday
stand tall and majestic
like a bodhisattva

*tetsupen yo tetsupen yo nare tada hitori waga utagai no areno ni
ugoku*

*yuki fureba kinō no hiru no waruhinoki bosatsu sugata ni suku to
tatsu kana*

at dawn
on a mountain pass
in the drifting fog
almost imperceptible
the smell of green tomatoes

in the blue rays
of opium light
falling from empty space
a lily's fragrance
rippling

akatsuki no tōge no kiri ni hosobosoto aoki tomato no nioi nagarenu

utsuro yori furikuru aoki ahenkō yuri no nioi wa namidachini tsutsu

silver greeting
exchanged between the sky
and the mountains
on a mountain farm
lush growth of millet

the plucked
feathers of a bird
glittering
like winged insects
fly away in the blue sky

*shirogane no aisatsu kawasu sora to yama yama no hatake wa hie
shigeri tsutsu*

*tori no ke wa mushirare tobite aozora ni hamushi no gotoku hikari
yuku kana*

River in Hell (two poems)

dead bodies adrift
on a phosphorescent stream
mingled with
some living people
swimming with their long arms

a head
severed from the body
grits its teeth
as it floats away
across the white stream

aojiroki nagare no naka wo shibito nagare hitobito nagaki ude mote oyogeri

atama nomi hito wo hanarete hagirishi shi shiroki nagare wo yogiri yuku nari

dark seaweeds
in the water's depths
every one of them
stretching misshapen arms
toward the radiant moon

emerging
amid the screams of clouds
in the sky
it flares up in a rage
a cypress

*minasoko no kuroki mo wa mina gekkō ni ayashiki ude wo
sashinoburu nari*

*amagumo no / wameki no naka ni waki idete / iradachi moyuru /
saipuresu kamo*

Ōkuma Nobuyuki

When Ōkuma Nobuyuki died on June 20, 1977, most of those who heard the news remembered him as an outspoken social critic who had taken bold stands on many controversial issues. A political science journal even published a special issue entitled "The Legacy of Ōkuma Nobuyuki." No literary magazine noted his passing, however. That was not surprising, for he had written no tanka for nearly forty years.

Nobuyuki was as devoted to writing verse in his early years as he was to social criticism later in life. Born on February 18, 1893, he began composing tanka when he was still a middle-school student in his home town of Yonezawa. He modeled his poetry on the work of Takuboku and Zenmaro. When Zenmaro founded the left-wing magazine *Seikatsu to geijutsu* in 1913, young Nobuyuki became a regular contributor. His interest in proletarian tanka was both strengthened and deepened by his study of Marxism as a student of economics at Tokyo Higher School of Commerce. He cofounded a poetry magazine in 1927 and published in it some of the earliest essays in defense of proletarian tanka in Japan. He was also a founding member of the League of Rising Tanka Poets, formed the following year. But his enthusiasm for writing left-wing tanka rapidly waned as the literary movement became more political. He began to turn his attention more toward formal innovation of tanka, exploring the possibilities of free-style tanka. From around the time he made a trip to Europe in 1929, his tanka grew longer in length and more irregular in prosody, until they became indistinguishable from ordinary free verse. At this point he lost many of his readers, until he stopped writing poetry in the mid-1930s.

In his professional career Nobuyuki taught economics at Toyama University, Kanagawa University, Sōka University, and elsewhere. He was a popular professor and was seen dancing with his students at discos even after he turned eighty. For some reason he was reluctant to bring out his poems in book form. *Ōkuma Nobuyuki kashū* (The Collected Tanka of Ōkuma Nobuyuki), published in 1931, was the only poetry collection that appeared during his lifetime; issued by a small publishing house in Yonezawa, it was not widely circulated. His other books, which number more than twenty, bear such titles as *Keizai honshitsu ron* (The Essence of Economics), *Bungei no Nihonteki keitai* (Japanese Types of Literature), *Kokka aku* (Evils of a Nation), and *Kekkonron to kateiron* (On Marriage and Homemaking)—a wide range of interests indeed.

Labor Day[1]
(four poems)

the cry of battle
rises up toward the sky
the surrounding
police troops
rest on the grass

calmly the citizens
watch the Labor Day
demonstrations
several hundreds of them
in the green shade

ŌKUMA NOBUYUKI   135

---

[1] Like English poems, Nobuyuki's tanka have titles. Following the waka tradition, tanka by most other poets bear no titles, although they are sometimes preceded by headnotes that explain the circumstances of composition.

toki no koe sora ni doyomitsu torikakomu keikantai wa kusa ni yasurau

mēdē wo mamoru shimin no shizukasa yo midori no kage ni ikusen ka iru

his arms
tightly grasped
from right and left
by the hands of policemen
swords on their waists

peddlar
pushing a cart
poor fellow!
in this huge
Labor Day crowd

136 ŌKUMA NOBUYUKI

moroude wo sayū ni kitsuku toraretari tsurugi hakitaru keikan no te ni

monouri no teoshiguruma no awaresa yo kono mēdē no hitogomi no naka

Even Invisible Things (two poems)

even invisible things
are all toppled over
things that have been buried under
begin to stand up

overturn
everything there is
one calls out
another calls out
all the echoes call out

ŌKUMA NOBUYUKI   137

mienu mono made   mina kutsugaeri   shitajiki to narishi mono
tachiagari kuru

kutsugaere   nani mo ka mo yo to   hitori yobu   mata hitori yobu
kodama mina yobu

Humans Bought and Sold
(two poems)

as the years pass
their laments grow
more and more feeble
those who still live
after their wings were clipped

no matter what this world
may become in the future
who is going to make amends
for those streaming tears?

*toshi hetsutsu   nageku kokoro mo   yowayowashi   tsubasa mogarete
nao ikeru mono*

*nochi ni yo wa   dō narō to mo   koko ni nagaruru muko no namida
wo   tare ka tsugunau*

Fiery Declarations
(two poems)

little by little
an overwhelming force
starts to roll
look! there appears
a new side

this far
you may advance
but not beyond
that's what they say

advance farther beyond!

ŌKUMA NOBUYUKI   139

*omomuroni   omoki chikara wa   kaiten shi   miyo atarashiki   men ga
arawaruru*

*soko made wa   yoshi to iinagara   sono saki wa   naranu to iu zo   sono
saki wo yuke*

And Then

I've always done so
I'll always do so
if I didn't do so
what else could I do?

Ashtray (two poems)

still a virgin
yet something has
grazed the skin
what could be done
about that face of yours?

*ore wa sō shite kita   korekara mo sō shite yuku   sō suru yori hoka ni
dō suru no da*

*shojo no mama   nani ka ni surimukarete   shimatte iru   anata no kao
wo   dō shitara yoi*

no matter how
beautiful it may look
an ashtray is where
everyone drops
his cigarette ends

In Berlin

two large dogs
being walked
by a man
hanging his head
whose servant?

.

*ikani kirei to itta tokoro de haizara wa suigara wo dare mo otosu
dake no mono*

*ōkina nihiki no inu wo ayumasete unadarete kuru no wa tare no
shimobe ka*

Stone Buddha
(two poems)

from where you are
a long
long
way off
I won't think of it
I never will
it makes me dizzy

                    didn't know
                    didn't understand
                    couldn't speak
                    didn't make a pledge
                    haven't given up

*anata e no harukana harukana hedatari wo omoumai omoumai
memai wo moyoosu*

*shiranakatta wakaranakatta ienakatta chikawanakatta
akiramenakatta*

Returning from Abroad

from the bucket's edge
a worm tumbled down
don't say a thing
went to a toilet
welcome back to Japan

Third-Class Car on a Night Train (three poems)

crumpled handkerchief
in one hand
with no baggage
slender legs exposed
standing near the door
swaying
and sighing from time to time

ŌKUMA NOBUYUKI   143

oke no fuchi kara   uji ga korogeta   nani mo iuna   kawaya ni haitta
Nippon ni kaetta

hankechi wo   te ni marume   mochimono wa nani mo nai   hosoi
suashi   irikuchi ni tatte yurarete   tokidoki tameiki tsuite.

the train rolls
the white breast sways
the baby frets
the eyes of a young man
sitting opposite
close and open

immovable in a seat
with his head down
an aged farmer sleeps
breathing
with his massive chest

kisha ga yure shiroi chibusa ga yure muzukaru akanbo mamukai
no wakamono no me ga tojite wa mata aku.

koshikaketa mama kubi wo tare mijiroganu rōnōfu no nemuri
ikizuite iru atsui munehaba.

Maekawa Samio

Except for writing tanka, Maekawa Samio engaged himself in no activity that could be called an occupation. In his later years he reflected on that fact and said: "Because I occupied myself with poetry, I could not do anything else that I had wanted to do." What that "anything else" was, he did not say. Probably he could not have said, since writing tanka was really all he wanted in life.

In his young days Samio had no financial reasons to work. Born on February 5, 1903, he was heir to a wealthy family that owned a huge area of land in Nara prefecture. The elementary school he attended as a child stood on land donated by his family. He began writing tanka as a sixth grader and continued doing so throughout his student days. He moved to Tokyo to attend Toyō University in 1922, and although he graduated from it three years later, he continued living in Tokyo in order to participate in the founding of the League of Rising Tanka Poets in 1928 and the Art School Tanka Club in 1930. His father's death in 1932, however, induced him to go back to Nara, get married, and assume the leadership of the Maekawa clan. This return to the ancient capital of Japan apparently inspired him with nationalism and, coupled with the wartime sentiments common at the time, he became associated with a group of nationalistic poets and writers. The titles of the poetry collections he published during the war—*Yamato* (Japan), *Tenpyōun* (The Clouds of Tenpyō), and *Yamato shi uruwashi* (Japan is Beautiful)— indicate his frame of mind. When the end of the war came in 1945, he had to face a crisis both financially and mentally. Under the Occupation Army's policy of equalizing land ownership, virtually all of the land owned by his family was appropriated by the government and redistributed to local farmers. The financial stress, his wife's illness, and critics' attacks on his wartime writings proved too much for him, and he fell into severe depression. Eventually he recovered, and from around 1953 he resumed writing tanka with renewed vigor, venting his anger and grief in language more realistic than before. He received a Shaku Chōkū Prize in 1971 and was inducted into the Japan Art Academy in 1989. He died of pneumonia on July 15, 1990.

reverently
placed on an altar
my head
the sight so unreal
I let myself watch it and cry

why does a room
have to be rectangular?
asking myself
I stare around the room
like a lunatic

*tokonoma ni matsurarete aru waga kubi wo utsutsu naraneba naite
mite ishi*

*nani yue ni heya wa shikaku de naranu ka to kichigai no yōni heya
wo mimawasu*

if only
I could clean out the inside
of my body
and stuff it with those
green leaves of daffodils!

surely by now
the empty wooden bathtub
left at my old home
must have begun to shoot out
pale vermilion mushrooms

mune no uchi ichido kara ni shite ano aoki suisen no ha wo
tsumekomite mitashi

furusato no munashi furo ni wa imagoro wa usushu no kinoko haeiru
to omou

because my room
is filled with the scent
of flowers
my thoughts on death have become
a little flowery

monumental
idiot that I am
I've sent an umbrella
to a bicycle shop
for repairs

MAEKAWA SAMIO   149

kusabana no nioi michiiru heya nareba sukoshi hanayakana shi wo omoitari

hijōnaru hakuchi no boku wa jitenshaya ni kōmorigasa wo shūzen ni yaru

on the sandy beach
a man with no eyes or nose
left forgotten
for how long
nobody can tell

no scar
found anywhere on my body
and yet
long ago I was born
out of my mother

*sunahama ni me mo hana mo nai ningen ga itsugoro kara ka
suterarete ari*

*nani hitotsu mi ni kizu nado wa motanakuni mukashi haha yori ware
wa umareki*

a loud voice
sounding like mine
calls me
as I hide in a tree
my body curled up

the day I was born
all the fields and hills
were in heavy fog
making it impossible
to see my mother

waga koe ni nishi ōki koe ga ware wo yobu ware chiisaku narite ki no
ue ni iru

umareta hi wa no mo yama mo fukai kasumi nite haha no sugata ga
mirarenakatta

when the gardener
turns on water
for the fountains
morning turns into
a peaceful park

memories open
like a peacock's feathers
alluring me
back to the island
of insatiable desire

*entei ga funsui no neji wo mawasu toki asa wa shizukana kōen to
naru*

*omoide wa kujaku no hane to uchihiraki akunaki tanran no shima ni
kaeramu*

for a moment
stop to imagine
those fierce eyes
of a cornered animal
cowering in the dark

a fish skeleton
bleached white in the winter rain
makes me wonder
what will be happening
at the end of this trail

*kuragari ni mi wo oshikakusu ikimono no susamajiki me wa hitotoki
omoe*

*fuyu no ame ni utaruru uo no hone shiroshi kono michi no hatate
nani ga aruramu*

in the evening wind
clusters of bush clover
start to blossom
revealing a path
my soul will follow

with each quiver
it is laying an egg
a white moth
why did it enter my mind
this frosty night?

yūkaze ni hagimura no hagi sakidaseba waga tamashii no tōrimichi miyu

furuetsutsu tamago umiiru shiroki ga wo kakaru shimoyo ni omou wa nani zo

on occasion
even a winged bird
has to scamper
like an animal in the grass
after spring has passed

call to mind
those men of the past
who died a happy death
each in a different way
how indomitable was their will!

*tobu tori mo kemono no gotoku kusa kuguri hashiru toki ari haru no
owari wa*

*samazama no yoki shini wo shite owaritaru mukashibito omoe mina
susamajiki*

on a starry night
I walk on the roof
till the end of time
I keep walking
on the slanted roof

with the blue
tail feather of a pheasant
torn up and eaten
at our dinner yesterday
I brush my desktop

*hoshi no yo wo yane no ue aruku kagiri naku katamuku yane no ue
aruki yuku*

*kinō ka mo sakite kuraeru yamadori no aoki oha mote tsukue wo
harau*

Saitō Fumi

In a postscript to one of her books of tanka, Saitō Fumi wrote: "As for the kind of poems that say I have traveled somewhere or met someone or walked along some muddy street in the rain, I have included few of them in this anthology." She has produced few such poems in her life anyway, as she has always been an anti-shasei poet who works with abstractions from nature and human life. Yet in her actual life she has gone on many journeys, befriended a number of people, and encountered more than her share of rainstorms.

Fumi was born in Tokyo on February 14, 1909, but her family moved to a different area of Japan each time her father, a high-ranking officer of the army, was transferred. He was also a respected tanka poet, and young Fumi became interested in that verse form while she helped with his verse-writing parties. She began publishing her tanka in magazines in 1926 and continued doing so after she married a physician in 1931 and settled down in Tokyo. In 1936, her father and some young officers she knew were accused of involvement in an army insurrection known as the February 26 Incident. After the insurrection was put down, several of the officers were found guilty and executed. Fumi gave birth to a daughter in that eventful year, and to a son in 1941. In 1945, as the air raids on Tokyo grew more devastating, she and her husband took refuge in the mountainous prefecture of Nagano in central Honshu. The family of four had to live in a barn for a couple of years. In 1953 they built their own house in the city of Nagano, and her husband opened a clinic there. She had been active as a poet all through those years, and did not slow down even after she began tending her mother, who became blind in 1968, and her husband, who became partially paralyzed in 1973. *Hitakurenai* (Entirely Crimson), a collection of tanka she wrote while nursing them both, won her a Shaku Chōkū Prize in 1977. *Watari ka yukamu* (I Will Cross Over), her next book of poetry, published in 1985, received a Yomiuri Literature Prize. In 1993, she was inducted into the Japan Art Academy. She has published nine books of tanka, a novel, a collection of essays, and an introduction to tanka-writing.

wood borers
eating deep into the growth rings
in the stillness
of a mountain where
trees are beginning to die

even the black gloves
I threw away in the field
start to rise
each of their fingers
shooting out a yellow flower

nenrin ni fukaku kuiiru mushi mo ite kodachi no kareru yama no
shizukesa

no ni suteta kuroi tebukuro mo okiagari yubiyubi ni ki na hana
sakasedasu

sweeter than a song
hummed in the evening dusk
sweeter than a rose
some wickedness beautifully
blooms inside my body

Turbid current

living at a time
when violence can look
so beautiful
I sing from morning till night
nothing but lullabies[1]

[1] The poem was written in 1936, shortly after the February 26 Incident.

tasogare no hanauta yori mo bara yori mo akuji yasashiku mi ni hanayaginu

bōryoku no kaku utsukushiki yo ni sumite hinemosu utau waga komoriuta

when I think over
what will happen to this body
after it perishes
a brook begins to murmur
somewhere far in the darkness

water streams
along the cracks of my skull
ages having gone by
since I lay down to sleep
at the bottom of a lake

horobitaru waga utsusomi wo omou toki kurayami tōku nagare no oto
su

waga zugai no hibi wo nagaruru mizu ga ari sudeni kotei ni inete
hisashiki

this huge pile
slowly decaying
on my unsteady back
are these
the fallen leaves of spring?

seeds of the grass
continually falling
before those
wholly unsuspecting lives
I kneel on the ground

*fuan naru waga se ni tsumite obitadashiku kuchitsutsu aru wa haru
no ochiba ka*

*kusa no mi wa koborete yamazu makasetaru inochi no mae ni te wo
tsukinikeri*

a white hare
that wandered out of the
snowy mountains
because it was slain
still keeps its eyes open

to take a bath
I go into the black water
of a lake
each time finding I am
followed by a drowned man

shiroki usagi yuki no yama yori idete kite korosaretareba me wo hiraki
ori

kuroki umi no mizu wo abimu to shizumu toki ware ni tsuki kuru
suishinin hitori

a palm of the hand
not knowing what it means
to die
becomes cold and hardened
and a little shrunken

don't resemble me
please don't—I tell the woman
I am painting
who has the beautiful
smile of an adulteress

*tenohira wa shi wo shiru koto nashi onozukara tsumetaku kataku
yaya chijimu nomi*

*ware ni niruna niruna to egaku sakuchū no onna utsukushiki fugi no
egao su*

crooked fireworks
though wiped off in an instant
leave behind
a heaven that will never
be without the scars

trailing for a while
behind my transparent body
after death
a string of tattered rags
that were once my tanka

yugamitaru hanabi tachimachi nuguedomo mukizu no sora to naru
koto wa nashi

tōmei to naritaru ware no shigo shibaraku sakishi boro no gotoku uta
hikizuramu

ever deeper
will be the doubt in my mind
with which I live
after witnessing a stain
on the white robe of a god

when neither a man
nor a horse is seen passing
over a bridge
only then it begins to show
what a true bridge is like

166   SAITŌ FUMI

*iyoiyo fukaku kokoro mayoite ikurubeshi kami no byakue no shimi mo
mite nochi*

*hito mo uma mo wataranu toki no hashi no kei makoto junsui ni
hashi kakariiru*

bones of a fish
licked until they have no more
smell of life
repose in white peace
amid a pile of garbage

in my possession
a picture book pierced through
by a bullet
I open it many times
before going to sleep

neburarete gyokotsu namagusa wo saritareba akuta no naka ni
hisomari shiroshi

dankon ga tsuranukishi issatsu no ehon ari nemuramu to shite
shibashiba hiraku

a cluster
of volcanic mountains
inside myself
slowly cool down as they must
with their crests missing

snow seeping
endlessly seeping
into a lake
that hides in its interior
a dark green universe

waga uchi ni aru kazangun itadaki no mina kakeshi mama hiyuru
hoka nashi

yuki ga shimu kagirinaku shimu mizuumi no sono naiō no anryoku
sekai

Miya Shūji

In his later years Miya Shūji had the nickname Miyan Shujinovich, because his face was covered with a grizzled beard that made him look like some figure out of Russian literature, which in fact he was fond of reading. Actually, growing a beard was not of his own choice; he became unable to shave after his rheumatism so advanced as to limit the movements of his hands. The smile on his bearded face was always warm and genuine, yet beneath it lay a life ridden with pain and hardship.

Miya Shūji, whose real name was Miya Hajime, was born on August 23, 1912, in the northern prefecture of Niigata. His father owned a bookstore and published a literary magazine, but since the business was slowly on the decline young Shūji had to work to help the family finances as soon as he graduated from middle school. At age twenty he left home for Tokyo, where he managed to survive by delivering newspapers and doing other miscellaneous work. His life became somewhat settled in 1935, when he was hired as a secretary by the poet Kitahara Hakushū. It was then that Shūji began writing tanka in earnest. But apparently his teacher's genius overwhelmed Shūji, who in 1939 gave up his poetic ambitions and found employment with Fuji Steel Company. Later in the same year he was drafted by the army and spent the next four years at the war front in northern China. Although he returned to Japan in 1943 and married the following year, he was recalled to active duty in 1945 and had to serve until the end of the war. In 1946 he published his first book of tanka, *Gunkei* (Flock of Chickens), which immediately brought him recognition. However, life was not easy for him in the chaotic postwar period, as he had to support his aged parents, wife, and two small children on his meagre salary from the steel company. He assumed further responsibilities in 1952, when his tanka group founded a magazine of their own. The title of his fourth book of tanka, *Banka* (Late Summer), already suggests awareness of his declining physical condition. In 1955 he had to be hospitalized for one month, marking the start of his bout with the many illnesses that tormented him for the rest of his life. In 1960 he retired from Fuji Steel so that he could devote more time to writing poetry. His work in those later years won him many honors, including a Yomiuri Literature Prize in 1961, a Shaku Chōkū Prize in 1975, and a Japan Academy of Art Prize in 1976. The Emperor bestowed a Purple Ribbon Medal on him in 1981, and his election to the Japan Academy of Art followed two years later. He died of heart failure on December 11, 1986.

red flowers
I saw on a silk tree
in the daytime
turn into my heart's desire
and haunt my mind at night

out of the shade
and toward the sunlight
a flock of chickens
with their numerous legs
walks on

hiruma mishi kōka no akaki hana no iro wo akogare no gotoku yoru omoi ori

hikage yori hi no teru kata ni muradori no kazu ōki ashi ayumite yuku mo

suddenly
in the midst of a battle
momentary calm
a chicken squawks
this terrible loneliness[1]

over my
slumbering body
a smeary
animal of night passes
as I let it pass

172   MIYA SHŪJI

[1] This and the following tanka were written at the front during the poet's military service
in China.

*tatakai no sanaka shizumoru toki arite niwatori nakeri osoroshiku
sabishi*

*nemurioru karada no ue wo yoru no kemono kegarete tōreri tōrashime
tsutsu*

flowering poppies
appear in my fantasy
and fill it with red
all things that have passed
touch my heart with sorrow

as if it came
to peer into my sorrow
a bronze-colored beetle
all alone
in the depth of night

MIYA SHŪJI 173

keshi no hana maboroshi ni kite akaku mitsu suginishi monora nabete
kanashi mo

kanashimi wo ukagau goto mo seidōshoku no kanabun hitotsu yowa
ni kite ori

spoken in response
some weakly intoned
Japanese words
a voice that has come
out of the dark Orient[2]

slanted
to some degree
this heart of mine
as I climb up a slope
bathed in the sunlight

[2] First published in 1948, the poem is part of a series on the Tokyo Trials, in which Japan's
wartime leaders were prosecuted by the Allies for war crimes. The poet listened to the
trials on the radio.

ōtō ni yokuyō hikuki Nihongo yo Tōyō no kurasa wo ayumi koshi koe

*ikubaku ka ware no kokoro no keisha shite hi ataru saka wo nobori
tsutsu ari*

after rainfall
in the luminous light
of the rising moon
their red still appears shady
flowers of a balsam

its bloom finished
a sunflower
heavy with black seeds
stands in the same posture
all day long in the garden

*ame no nochi noboreru tsuki no tereredomo kurenai wa kurashi yo no
hōsenka*

*hana oete kuroki mi taruru himawari wa onaji shisei ni hitohi niwa ni
tatsu* ·

slowly inside me
a thought has hardened
into a belief
world peace will never
be nature's gift

During the rainy season

there float away
straws and rubbish and all
looking as if
bound for eternity
on the water's surface

176   MIYA SHŪJI

jojoni jojoni kokoro ni narishi omoi hitotsu shizenzai naru heiwa wa arazu

nagaretsutsu wara mo akuta mo eien ni mukau ga gotoku mizu no mo ni ari

stalks growing
straight, green and sharp
a forest of bamboos
occasionally with something
that makes me panic

like a long
flame of a candle
flickering
and flaring up for a moment
my youth has come and gone

*mikidachi no aoku surudoku takemure wa aru oriori ni obiyakashi
motsu*

*rōsoku no nagaki honoo no kagayakite yuretaru gotoki wakaki yo
suginu*

Mr. Nehru
and Mr. Malenkov
strangely
come to my mind together
as the day begins to dawn

The year's end

without end
they keep appearing
in my illusion
those animals that leap
and leap again as they pass

*Nēru-shi to Marenkofu-shi wo fushigi ni mo narabe omoite itaru
akegata*

*hōzu naku waga mōzōri ni arawarete chōyaku shi chōyaku shi
kedamonora sugu*

on the way home
from where I work for a living
I stop to watch
vegetables at a grocer's
being sprayed with water

to do away with anger
my mind wanders far
to the end of the earth
a white continent
on the dark green waters

seikatsu no kyō no kaeriji mitsutsu tatsu mizu utareyuku yaoya no yasai

ikari wo ba shizumen to shite chi no hate no shirotairiku anryokukai wo shinobi itariki

at a corner
of the breezy arbor
wisteria plumes
caressing one another
in purple darkness

my body
wasting away in sickbed
this sorrow
resembles an old leaf
fallen from a loquat tree

*kaze kayou tana ichigū ni fusabana no fuji momiaeba murasaki no
yami*

*sutaretaru karada yokotae biwa no ki no furuki ochiba no gotoki
kanashimi*

Kondō Yoshimi

Kondō Yoshimi calls two places his hometown, and both profoundly affect his outlook on life, constantly reminding him of the formidable power a government has over the life of an individual. One is a small town in Korea where he was born. The other is Hiroshima, where he lived as a youngster for nine years. In Korea he saw the plight of Koreans under the Japanese rule. Luckily, he was elsewhere when Hiroshima was destroyed by atomic bombing.

Yoshimi was born on May 5, 1913, as the oldest son of a Japanese bank employee stationed in Korea. When he was twelve, his parents sent him to his grandmother's home in Hiroshima so that he could attend middle school in Japan. Because several teachers at the school were tanka poets, he began writing tanka under their guidance. His interest in poetry did not wane even after he entered Tokyo College of Engineering in 1935 and chose architecture for his area of specialization. The engineering diploma he earned in 1938 landed him a job with Shimizu Construction Company, which promptly transferred him to its branch office in Seoul. In 1940 he married a young tanka poet and daughter of a professor at Seoul University, but two months later he was drafted by the army and sent to China. Near the Yangtze River he was wounded in the leg. During treatment his doctors discovered tuberculosis and had him sent back to Japan. Soon he recovered well enough to resume working at Shimizu Construction's headquarters in Tokyo, but the capital city was by then not unlike a battlefield because of nightly air raids. Throughout this difficult period he had continued to write tanka, most of which, however, could not be published until after the war. When they finally appeared in 1948 in two books entitled *Sōshunka* (Songs of Early Spring) and *Hokori fuku machi* (Streets Where Dust Swirls), Yoshimi was recognized as a leading tanka poet of the postwar period. His life from that point on has been less dramatic, though no less productive in both of his careers. As an architect, he was awarded a doctor of engineering degree in 1961 and became a professor of engineering at Kanagawa University upon his retirement from Shimizu Construction in 1973. As a poet, he received a Shaku Chōkū Prize in 1969 and has been on the editorial staff of the tanka magazine, *Mirai* (Future), since its inception in 1951. With more free time in his later years, he has traveled all over the world, and has published sixteen books of tanka so far.

having crushed
on my drawing paper
a fallen gnat
I wipe off the stain with bread
the following morning

because
I tore up the photograph
and tossed it in
a fish floats up to the surface
from the blue depths

ochite kishi hamushi wo tsubuseru seizushi no yogore wo pan de fuku
akuru asa ni

hikisakite ware sutenikeru shashin yue aoki soko yori uo ukite izu

a spoon
near my pillow
swarms with ants
I kill them all
in the middle of the night

having grown up
in a culture devoid
of religion
inspired by what faith
am I to fight this war?[1]

KONDŌ YOSHIMI

[1] This and the following poem were written while the poet was in military service in China.

makurabe no saji ni muragari itarikeru yonaka no ari wo ware wa koroseri

shūkyō wo kyōyō to senu yo ni sodachi tatakai yukeba nani shinjikemu

scissors
cut through my bloodstained
military uniform
with a snipping sound
that is repeated a while

along a street
under the still misted sky
after a shower
someone carrying on his back
a transparent glass pane

chi no tsukishi ware no gun'i wo sakinagara hasami wa shibashi oto wo tatetsutsu

furi sugite mata kumoru machi sukitōru garasu no ita wo oite ayumeri

the ocean
gleams like mercury
in the distance
as I work inside our office
with a raincoat on [2]

since I work with those
who don't speak my language
this empty feeling
I go out and buy a copy
of the *Communist Manifesto* [3]

[2] Because office buildings had no heating facilities in the postwar period, even those who worked indoors had to wear overcoats in order to keep themselves warm in winter.
[3] On his company's orders, the poet worked at an Occupation Army base in Tokyo for a period of time in 1945.

suigin no gotoki hikari ni umi miete reinkōto wo kiru heya no naka

kotoba shirazu hataraki aeba hakanaki ni idete kyōsantō-sengen wo kau

with headlights on
a line of bulldosers
bound for home
comes out of a building site
in the lowering blizzard

the moment
another window is broken
we all laugh
resuming the next moment
faces devoid of expression[4]

KONDŌ YOSHIMI   187

---

[4] Another scene in postwar Japan. Trains were so overpacked with passengers that it was not uncommon to see a window broken accidentally.

hi tomoshite kaeru haidoki tsuranarite fubuki to narishi sagyōba wo izu

madogarasu wareshi isshun mata warai sudeni warera ni hyōjō mo naki

soldiers on the ground
swept with gunfire from the air
again and again
through the entire sequence
the audience sits in silence [5]

casting shadows
on the white riverbed
heavy bombers descend
each looking as though
not a soul were on board

[5] Written in 1950, after the outbreak of the Korean War.

kurikaeshi chijō no gun wo sōsha suru gamen no aida tsuzuku
chinmoku

ishi shiroki kawara ni kage shi orite yuku jūbakuki mina hito aranu
goto

a streetcar
shrouded in an instant
by the whirling snow
in the darkling metropolis
as I watch from a window

The white sky[6]

their voice that cursed
has now become the voice
of the weak
thanks to magnanimity
brought by the passage of time

[6] The headnote refers to the white mushroom clouds that rose in the sky above Hiroshima after the atomic bomb attack in 1945. Those who survived suffered from various ill effects for the rest of their lives. The poem was written in 1957.

densha ichidai hayaku fubuki ni tsutsumaruru machi mieteori kururu mado yori

juso no koe ima wa jakushara no koe to shite saigetsu ga mata yurushi yuku mono

how many people came
to Pasternak's funeral
she told me
but didn't answer my question
a woman teacher one night[7]

the street
holding the world's wealth
and its ambitions
extends in hushed silence
like a path through the graveyard[8]

190   KONDŌ YOSHIMI

[7] Written during a tour of the Soviet Union in 1961. Boris Pasternak had died in 1960, two years after being forced to decline a Nobel Prize.
[8] Written on Wall Street in New York during a U.S. tour in 1962.

Pasuterunāku hōmuri tsudoishi kazu tsugete kotae sezariki aru yo no jokyōshi

sekai no tomi atsumete tomi no ishi himuru machi no hisokesa wa bochi wo yuku goto

white jet clouds
trailing above the jungle
and then the bombing
no count for the victims
because they are peasants[9]

a dream
about the dark sky of dawn
where a god weeps
over the putrid smell
that spreads to the end of space

[9] This and the following two poems were written in 1965, during the Vietnam War.

mitsurin no sora shiroku yuku bakugeki ni nōmin nareba shisha wo kazoezu

yume wa kuraki sora no akatoki kagiri naki shishū no ue ni namida nagasu kami

gloomy rain
that soaks through the country
something that drives
a race to fight this war
with hardly a word spoken

Trip to Berlin

as divided
I never think of Germany
his words so calm
I couldn't tell whether they came
out of anger or sorrow[10]

[10] The poet visited the divided Germany during his European tour of 1969.

utsuutsuto kuni hitasu ame ichiminzoku wo kakaru kamoku ni
tatakawashimuru mono

bunkatsu sareshi Doitsu to omowazu to kikeru imi shizuka nareba
ikari ka hiai ka shirazu

Tsukamoto Kunio

Most major tanka poets active in the twentieth century started their writing careers under one teacher or another and associated with members of the tanka club led by that teacher. Tsukamoto Kunio did not. As a result, hardly anyone in tanka circles paid attention to his first book of tanka, *Suisō monogatari* (The Tale of Burial at Sea), when it appeared in 1951. But lavish praise came from a maverick novelist, Mishima Yukio, who wrote a letter to the young poet that said, in part: "You have restored an important part of Japanese aesthetic sensibility that had been forgotten in modern Japan." Kunio's talent, like Mishima's own, proved too brilliant to remain in obscurity for long. Eventually his reputation as a tanka poet rose and reached the level of Mishima's as a novelist.

Tsukamoto Kunio is his real name. He was born on August 7, 1922, in Shiga prefecture. He was expected to enter the business world and so received education at Hikone College of Commerce, but personally he was more interested in poetry, painting, calligraphy, film, and music. In 1942 he was drafted into the navy, and although he was not sent on operations he did see a number of people killed when the naval port where he was stationed was attacked from the air. After the war ended in 1945 he found employment at a large commercial firm, where he worked until his retirement in 1974. He married in 1947 and had a son the following year, but this peaceful life was interrupted in 1954 when he contracted tuberculosis and spent the next two years recuperating. His activities

as a tanka poet, which had started during the war, re-
sumed with added fervor after the illness, resulting in
the publication of four books between 1956 and 1965.
Beginning in the 1970s he also wrote short stories and
novels, some of them featuring such historical figures as
Emperor Gotoba, Leonardo da Vinci, and Jesus Christ.
Simultaneously he displayed his acute critical sense by
publishing highly perceptive readings of waka, tanka, and
haiku. His *Mokichi shūka* (Superior Poems of Saitō Mo-
kichi), published in three volumes between 1977 and
1981, is one of the best books of tanka criticism ever
written. With his superabundant energy he has also com-
posed considerable numbers of haiku, renku, and son-
nets. The number of books that bear his name is well
over one hundred, and he has not yet shown any sign of
slowing down.

in a grove
of champagne bottles
someone teaching a class
on differential and integral
investment calculus

hands picking a rose
hands holding a shotgun
hands fondling a loved one
hands on every clock
point to the twenty-fifth hour

shanpan no bin no hayashi no kage de toku bibun sekibunteki
chochikugaku

bara tsumu te · jū sasaeru te · aiidaku te · te. . . no tokei ga sasu
nijūgo-ji

woman
like the barrel of a gun
I keep loading her
with liquid explosive
till the night is gone

                                        hidden
                                        inside the steel machine
                                        that is sewing
                                        her wedding dress
                                        a dark gadget

196   TSUKAMOTO KUNIO

jūshin no yōna onna ni yo no akeru made ekijō no kayaku tsumeiki

*kekkon ishō nui tsuzuriyuku kōtetsu no mishin no naka no kuraki
karakuri*

all the way
from the rooftop zoo
to the basement bar
a black water pipe
pierces the building

late summer day
in a country on the brink
of collapse

a nail buried in asphalt
shows its sparkling head

TSUKAMOTO KUNIO   197

okujō no jūen yori chika sakaba made kuroki suidōkan tsuranukeri

*kuni horobitsutsu aru banka   asufaruto ni maibotsu shitaru kugi no
zu hikaru*

even while
a comic movie is shown
it is right there
leaking cold beams of light
an emergency exit

from a flour mill
to a charity hospital
then to a butcher's
power lines extend
till they reach the withered moor

*kigeki eiga miteiru toki mo sugu soko ni tsumetaki hikari moru
hijōguchi*

seifunsho yori nobishi densen, jizenbyōin to nikuya wo tsunagi kareno e

because the folks
who were saved by death
sleep here
a graveyard in the dark
smells of moonlight

only when
the power is cut off
it begins to sing
a voiceless song of its own
the electric guitar

TSUKAMOTO KUNIO   199

*shi ni yorite sukuwareshi mono nemuru yue hakahara kuraku tsuki
niou kana*

denryū wo tatare, hajimete mizukara no koe naki uta utau denki gitā

a casket on display
at the mortuary
coldly
rests in peace
exactly matching my size

as night falls
on this early summer day
his forehead shiny
an insurance salesman
comes to sell a distant death

sōgiten no mihon no nekan samuzamuto ansoku ni michi ware to tōshin

hatsunatsu no yūbe hitai wo hikarasete hokenya ga tōki shi wo uri ni kuru

on the snow
after a shower has passed
thousands of rifles
hidden underground
aiming at heaven

stalwartly
youngsters strut
toward death
in the summer mountains
where ropes hang like intestines

yuki no ue wo shūu sugishi ga sūsen no chika yori ten ni mukeshi jūkō

*araarashiku shi e tōzakaru seinenra natsuyama ni chō no gotoki tsuna
tari*

after death
always a fresh tomorrow

brand new water
gurgling into a tank
at the aquarium

this May Day night
on the wet pavement
a beetle and I
one pretending to be dead
the other doing the reverse

*shi no nochi mo asu wa atarashi gobogoboto nettai akariumu no
mizu kawaru*

*Mēdē yo no michi nurete hanmyō wa shi wo yosooi ware wa sei wo
yosoou*

on the cloudy water
beyond the land of Asura
where I suffer
lotuses are blooming
with their pink alliterations[1]

on the water
floats a dead warbler
with its eyes closed
its beautiful days of shame
having passed and gone

TSUKAMOTO KUNIO   203

[1] In the Buddhist universe, the land of Asura is a sphere located between paradise and
various types of hell. The lotus is the flower of paradise.

*waga Shura no kanata kumoreru mizu no ue ni akaki tōin no hana
hiraku hasu*

*mizu no ue ni shi no uguisu no mami tojite haji utsukushiki hibi wa
sugitari*

standing still
in the twilight of a cold
spring evening
I wonder if a soul does not
resemble a leaf of gold

I've swept away
all the dust of literature
and yet
in a corner of my room
there's still a Gobi Desert

yokan yūgure awaki hikari ni tatsu ware ya konpaku wa kinpaku no tagui ka

bungaku no chiri hakisutete nao ware no heya no ichigū naru Gobi sabaku

Nakajō Fumiko

Nakajō Fumiko is one of the few Japanese poets who have had their lives made into a bestselling novel or a full-length commercial movie. Unfortunately, she did not live long enough to see either the book or the film. Her tragic life had ended years before they came out.

She was born Noe Fumiko on November 25, 1922, in the city of Obihiro on the northern island of Hokkaido. Her family, which owned and operated a fabric store, was affluent enough to send her to Tokyo for postsecondary education. In 1942 she married Nakajō Hiroshi, a bright young engineer working for the National Railways, and gave birth to three children in the next six years. The marital relationship had, however, become strained by the time the third child was born, largely because of her husband's drinking and drug problems. Apparently he was also involved in an affair with another woman. Finally in 1950 Fumiko left him, taking two of the children with her. Back at her parents' home, she was financially secure but emotionally unfulfilled, which led to romantic relationships with several young men. One of them, to whom she was especially close, died of tuberculosis. In 1952 cancer was discovered in her left breast. Immediately she had it removed by surgery, but the cancer had already spread to other parts of her body. Her right breast was operated on in late 1953. The following January she entered a hospital in Sapporo, from which she was never to come out alive. She died on August 3, 1954.

Fumiko had tried her hand at tanka composition during her student days in Tokyo, but had never taken it seriously until her married life became intolerable. She joined a local group of tanka poets in 1946 and began having her works published in little magazines. All of a sudden, however, she found herself a famous poet in April 1954, when a group of fifty poems written by her won the first prize in a nationwide tanka contest sponsored by a major magazine. Two months later, another prestigious journal published fifty-one tanka of hers, with a preface by the novelist Kawabata Yasunari. In July, her first book of tanka came out in Tokyo. The title was *Chibusa sōshitsu* (A Breast Lost), a phrase coined by analogy to *Rakuen sōshitsu* (Paradise Lost). A prepublication copy had to be rushed to her bedside, as she lay dying. She never saw her second book, *Hana no genkei* (The Prototype of Flowers), which appeared in April 1955.

boxes of sleeping pills
stacked up beside him
day in and day out
my husband sleeps in
unapproachable wretchedness

the eyes
of a cornered animal
and my husband's eyes
in my memory
merge for a moment

adorumu no hako kai tamete hibi nemuru otto no kōsan ni chikayori gatashi

oitsumerareshi kedamono no me to otto no me to shibashi kioku no naka ni kasanaru

the yellow bus
bound for a suburb
where my husband lives
this morning carries
a gift of hatred from me

my arms
holding a child
like the harvest of sorrow
feel a weight
far too heavy to measure

otto no sumu kōgai-yuki no ki no basu ni aru asa wa noseyaru ware
no zōo wo

kanashimi no minori no gotoki ko wo dakite sono omotasa wa kagiri
mo aranu

sharing the gentleness
two unrelated beings feel
toward each other
a grazing cow and I
in the setting sun

although blooming
untouchably white
it is a flower
and so will not look down on
my impurity

NAKAJŌ FUMIKO   209

muen naru mono no yasashisa mochiaite kusa hamu ushi to ware to
no higure

furegataku shiroku saku tomo hana nareba ware no fujō wo iyashime
wa sezu

in a posture
ready to leap
the animal waits
I walk toward him
ready to be slain

with a thunderous crack
flowers of fire open
in the night sky
leaving no part of my body
protected from the pillage

chōyaku no shisei ni kemono wa machi itari hōraremu to shi ware wa
chikazuku

oto takaku yozora ni hanabi uchihiraki ware wa kuma naku
ubawareteiru

each year
it dies out and then
blooms beautifully again
that flower's prototype
lies inside my body

as the surgical knife
slowly slits open
the past
my fetuses appear
kicking each other in the dark

toshidoshi ni horobite katsu wa atarashiki hana no genkei wa waga uchi ni ari

mesu no moto hirakarete yuku kako ga ari waga taijira wa yami ni keriau

in search of a shore
where I might spot my breast
drifting along
with white jellyfish
I'll go to sleep again

one day I saw
a rope hanging from a black
leafless tree
yet my hanged body
was nowhere to be seen

shiroki kurage ni majirite ware no chibusa uku kishi wo sagasamu
mata mo nemurite

kuroki hadakagi no eda ni himo nado mienagara kubireshi ware wa
orazaru aru hi

didn't a certain woman
who looked like me
have her breast cut off
for committing adultery
millenniums ago?

that hill
shaped like the breast
I have lost
will be adorned with
dead flowers in winter

ware ni nishi hitori no onna furin nite chichisogi no kei ni awazarishi ya kodai ni

ushinaishi ware no chibusa ni nishi oka ari fuyu wa karetaru hana ga kazaramu

wiggling out
from a fragile part
of myself
and swimming with its long fins
a red goldfish

knees collapsing
slowly she falls to the ground
in jest
that is another kind of ending
within my field of vision

214   NAKAJŌ FUMIKO

waga uchi no moroki bubun wo yuriidete hire nagaku oyogu akaki
kingyo wa

yukkurito hiza wo orite taoretaru asobi no gotoki shūmatsu mo mie

with sorrow I recall
young leaves on a cherry tree
as I lie face down
showing my back that has
not a single scar as yet

since that evening
when I first smelled the stench
of my dead body
the sharp eyes of a vulture
remain forever in my mind

hazakura no kioku kanashimu utsubuse no ware no senaka wa mada mukizu nari

ware to waga fushū wo kagishi yūbe yori taka no surudoki me wa tsukimatou

for this
insomniac of a woman
the night offers
a toad, a black dog
a drowned man and the like

                    when the lights go out
                    it comes sneaking in
                    and lies down next to me
                    I've tamed it so thoroughly
                    it feels like a comfort now

*fumin no ware ni yo ga yōi shi kuru mono gama, kuroinu, suishinin
no tagui*

*hi wo keshite shinobiyaka ni tonari ni kuru mono wo keraku no
gotoku ni ima wa narashitsu*

Sasaki Yukitsuna

"At my home, all the conversations are carried in 5-7-5-7-7." That is of course a joke, but Sasaki Yukitsuna was brought up in the kind of family that makes the joke sound true. Both his parents were tanka poets, and his home doubled as the editorial office of a venerable tanka magazine, *Kokoro no hana* (Flowers of the Heart), of which his father was editor. His grandfather and great-grandfather were renowned for their thirty-one-syllable verse. When he was a small child, his grandfather would give him candies as a reward for saying something in 5-7-5-7-7.

Yukitsuna was born in Tokyo on October 8, 1938. The obstetrician who helped with the delivery was the famous haiku poet Mizuhara Shūōshi. The family spurred him to learn the craft of tanka early, and he had his poems published in *Kokoro no hana* when he was six or seven years old. In high school he was more interested in playing basketball and rugby, but resumed writing tanka after he entered Waseda University. He majored in Japanese and completed the master's degree requirements in 1966. Those days were a peak period of student activism in Japan, and Yukitsuna often joined his classmates in political demonstrations. From 1966 to 1969 he worked at the editorial office of a publishing house in Tokyo, and in 1974 he took over the editorship of *Kokoro no hana*. He also launched his career as a college teacher, first at Waseda University in 1973 and then at Atomi Women's College two years later. He also has worked as a critic, essayist, lecturer on TV, and tanka editor for several major newspapers. So far he has published seven books of tanka, including *Gunrei* (The Multitude), which received a prize from the Association of Modern Tanka Poets in 1970, *Konjiki no shishi* (The Golden Lion), which was honored with a Museum of Japanese Poetry Prize in 1989, and *Taki no jikan* (The Hour of the Waterfall), which won a Shaku Chōkū Prize in 1994.

At the zoo (two poems)

an antelope
that doesn't gallop
and a man who doesn't hunt
understand each other
and avert their eyes

black leopard
a little overweight
scampers onto a tree
with no killing to perform
her daily life obscene

SASAKI YUKITSUNA   219

hashiranai kamoshika to ryō wo senu otoko wakariai tsutsu me wo sorasu nari

futorigimi no kurohyō ga ki wo kakenoboru satsugai nasanu nichijō midara

writing a series
of chemical formula
climaxed with an
imaginary explosion
all I did this afternoon

Baker's prayer

glory be to those
who eat the bread
baked by me!
I do not live
by bread alone

kagaku kigō kaki tsuraneyuki maboroshi no bakuhatsu togeshi nomi
kyō no gogo

ware no yakishi pan kuu yatsura ni eikō are! ware wa pan nomi ni
ikuru ni arazu

the moonlight
made me act so crazy
she lied to me
but I'm a coward too
and living with her now

with a hangover
I dip my body deep
into the bathtub
yet like grease or something
my shame refuses to sink

gekkō ni kuruishi to uso wo iu shōjo sono hikyō wo ba kyōyū shi iku

futsukayoi no karada wo furo ni shizume tsutsu shizume ezu abura no gotoki haji wa mo

always loving
progressive verb forms
I'm living near a river
and gazing once a day
at the reeking stream

overtaken by time
that stops at nothing
my train
that stopped for a minute
issues a shrill scream

222   SASAKI YUKITSUNA

*shinkōkei wo konomeba kawa ni chikaku sumi yogoreshi kawa wo hi
ni ichido miru*

*tomarazaru jikan ni nukare himei agu ippun teishago no waga kisha
wa*

since puberty
the son's voice has become
just like the father's
the resemblance especially
clear when they quarrel

poetry
is a midsummer mirror
with a fiery forehead
held close
in the darkening world

henseiki koete nite kishi fushi no koe aiarasoeru toki kiwadachishi

*shiika to wa manatsu no kagami, hi no nuka wo oshiatete tatsu
kururu sekai ni*

a youngster
coming aboard with a
caged cicada
becomes the focus of our
speeding bus on the night road

the bloom finished
trees stand above the petals
fallen on the ground
contemporary tanka
starts from that sight

*semi no kago wo motte norikishi shōnen wo shōten to shite hashiru yo
no basu*

*chiri oeshi hana shikite tatsu kigi no kage, gendai tanka wa sore kara
no uta*

with those who
have gathered to mourn
a friend's death
I look up toward the rope
hanging from heaven

changing
the blade of my razor
I contemplate
the skin of a young woman
I am to meet this afternoon

SASAKI YUKITSUNA   225

tomo no shi ni tsudoeru monora ware mo mata ten yori taruru nawa
wo miagete

kamisori no kaeba kaetsutsu omoeraku gogo ni au wakaki josei no
hadae

a plaintive
song of rain I knew
by heart
is gone from memory
as my sorrow is gone

during a trip
I lost my camera
after taking
snapshots of a beautiful
woman at springtime

226   SASAKI YUKITSUNA

*soranjite kanashiki ame no uta nariki kanashimi wa ase kashi mo
wasurenu*

*tabisaki ni ushinaitarishi kamera kana haru no bijin wo utsushitarishi
ga*

each morning I awake
with a dream of someone
in hot pursuit of me
I am a plump
middle-aged giraffe

beyond doubt
one was my fancy's
concoction
a hawk of yesterday
a hawk I saw today

SASAKI YUKITSUNA   227

owaruru yume mitsutsu sametaru kinō kyō ware wa chūnen no koetaru kirin

izure ka ichiwa waga maboroshi to utagawazu kinō no taka to kyō mitaru taka

amid the waves of time
rich in primary colors
my drifting soul
I pull it to the shore
at two in the morning

child in my arms
before a tiger's cage
I stand
dressed in the leather garments
of peaceful life

genshoku no jikan namidachi fuyū suru kokoro wo kishi ni hiku gozen niji

ko wo daite tora no iru ori no mae ni tatsu heion no kawagoromo kite ware wa

Tawara Machi

When Tawara Machi was born on December 31, 1962, most of her family members wanted to wait for one day before having her birth officially registered. Not only did January 1 seem a more auspicious day for a birthday, but 1962 was the Year of the Tiger, and it was popularly believed that girls born during that year would frighten boys away when they reached marriageable age. However, the matter was of no concern to Machi's father, a physicist, who went ahead and reported her birthdate as it was. His action was prophetic, because the baby grew up to become an eloquent spokesperson for *shinjinrui* or "new human species," a generation of Japanese who show little concern for traditional beliefs, even for the traditional institution of marriage.

Machi spent her childhood in Osaka. When she was fourteen, her family moved to a small town near Fukui and she attended high school there. Her main extracurricular activity in those days was acting, and she often appeared on the stage in the school's drama productions. She had little interest in poetry until she entered Waseda University in Tokyo and took one of the courses given by Sasaki Yukitsuna in her junior year. The charms of tanka caught her immediately, enticing her to write a senior thesis on the art of arranging tanka in sequence. She also began to write poems herself and joined the *Kokoro no hana* group in 1983. Just a few months later, she was surprised and encouraged to find her name on the list of finalists for the Kadokawa Tanka Prize. In 1985 she graduated from Waseda and began teaching Japanese at Hashimoto High School in Kanagawa prefecture, but her teaching career lasted only for four years. That was because her first book of tanka, *Sarada kinenbi* (Salad Anniversary) became a major bestseller almost as soon as it appeared in 1987, causing "the Tawara phenomenon" and making her a much-wanted person on TV and at the lectern. "My first tanka collection was initially a heaven-sent shower of rain for me, but at some point it turned into a storm and almost blew me away," she recollected. She stood firm in her path, however, and published her second book of tanka, *Kaze no tenohira* (The Palm of the Wind), in 1991. Beyond doubt, many more books of tanka will follow.

gazing upwards
toward the falling rain
suddenly
I long to be kissed
in this very stance

loneliness
of life where one and one
always make two
showers down on me
this December day

*ochite kita ame wo miagete sono mama no katachi de fui ni,
kuchibiru ga hoshi*

*ichi purasu ichi wo ni to shite ikite yuku sabishisa ware ni furu
jūnigatsu*

"Until age thirty
I'm going to take a stroll"
your words
make me wonder what part
of your scenery I am

this day in March
with no part of my heart
waiting for spring
I gaze with you
at a late blossoming plum

"30 made burabura suruyo" to iu kimi no ikanaru fūkei na no ka
watashi wa

haru wo matsu kokoro wo motanu sangatsu ni osozaki no ume kimi to
miteiru

the letter
overflows with love
the love
that is what it was
on the day of the postmark

from the moment
I finish writing
and put a stamp
time begins to flow
waiting for an answer

tegami ni wa ai afuretari sono ai wa keshiin no hi no sono toki no ai

kakioete kitte wo hareba tachimachini henji wo matte toki nagaredasu

trying to wash away
the dust that has gathered
from what they saw
I rinse my contact lenses
as thoroughly as I can

cherry blossoms
cherry blossoms cherry blossoms
start blooming
end blooming and the park looks
as if nothing had happened

mishi koto no nigori wo arai nagasu goto kontakuto renzu tsuyoku susugeru

sakura sakura sakura sakisome sakiowari nani mo nakatta yōna kōen

on a day
when I forget to hear
the morning forecast
I don't get upset
be it rain or shine

my heart
wishing to turn white
for a time
goes out to a musing lily
and keeps its company

*tenki yohō kikinogashitaru ichinichi wa ame de mo hare de mo hara
ga tatanai*

*shibaraku wa shiroku naritaki kokoro ari yuri no kangaegoto ni
tsukiau*

as though to let loose
all the chains binding him
to society
he takes off the suit jacket
the tie, the trousers, the white shirt

the woman
who gave birth to your child
has a smile on her face
her eyebrows, lips and all
the night of a crescent moon

*shakai to no kusari wo hodoku yōni nugu sebiro, nekutai, zubon,
waishatsu*

*kimi no ko wo umeru nyonin no hohoemi no mayuge mo kuchi mo
mikazuki no yoru*

although
not thick enough to be called
hatred
there's some opaque liquid
accumulating in my chest

freezing my smile
for half a second
I look
toward your camera
that can't photograph my heart

zō to iu hodo no nōdo wo motanu mama torori to mune ni nani ka tamareru

nibun no ichibyō egao wo tomete kimi wo miru watashi no kokoro wa utsusenu kamera

arriving
a little later than usual
and leaving me
disappointed as usual
the mailman

only the green
among my colored pencils
has become short
suggesting the color
I am deficient in

238   TAWARA MACHI

itsumo yori yaya osoku kite itsumo dōri gakkari sasete yuku
posutoman

iroenpitsu no midori bakari ga hetteiru ware ni tarinai iro ka mo
shirezu

looking as though
their ears were attuned to
the ocean's rumble
daffodils are in bloom
at the village where I was born

with a serene look
seen only after childbirth
an apple tree
opens its hands wide
to welcome the snow season

TAWARA MACHI   239

uminari ni mimi wo sumashite iru yōna suisen no hana hiraku
furusato

umioeshi nochi no sugashisa ringoju wa ryōte wo hiroge yuki wo
mukaeru

all the more
because it cannot be seen
I gaze forever
toward the land said to be
lying beyond the ocean

somehow this impulse
to ask about your birthplace
as I walk with you
through a dusky hallway
at the aquarium

*mienu kara nao itsu made mo mite orinu umi no mukō ni aru hazu
no kuni*

furusato no koto wo kikitashi honoguraki suizokkan no tsūro yuku toki

Selected Bibliography

This bibliography is limited to publications in English. Under "Individual Poets" each poet's tanka available in translation are listed first, followed by his or her writings in other genres. Biographical and critical studies of the poet appear last.

1. History and Criticism

Keene, Donald. "The Creation of Modern Japanese Poetry." In his *Landscapes and Portraits*. Tokyo: Kodansha International, 1971.

———. "The Modern Tanka." In his *Dawn to the West*. New York: Holt, Rinehart & Winston, 1984.

Japan P.E.N. Club, "Tanka." In Japan P.E.N. Club, *A Survey of Japanese Literature Today*. Tokyo: Japan P.E.N. Club, 1984.

Okazaki, Yoshie. "The Reformation of Tanka and Its Development." In his *Japanese Literature in the Meiji Era*, trans. by V. H. Viglielmo. Tokyo: Obunsha, 1955.

2. Individual Poets

ISHIKAWA TAKUBOKU
Tanka in Translation
Bownas, Geoffrey and Anthony Thwaite, trans. Thirteen poems, in their *The Penguin Book of Japanese Verse*. Baltimore: Penguin Books, 1964.

Carter, Steven D., trans. Eight poems, in his *Traditional Japanese Poetry*. Stanford: Stanford University Press, 1991.

Evans, Unity, trans. Three poems, in Roger Bersihand, *Japanese Literature*. New York: Walker, 1965.

Goldstein, Sanford and Seishi Shinoda, trans. *Sad Toys*. West Lafayette, Ind.: Purdue University Press, 1977.

Honda, H. H., trans. *The Poetry of Ishikawa Takuboku*, Tokyo: Hokuseido, 1959.

Keene, Donald, trans. Five poems, in his *Dawn to the West.*
New York: Holt, Rinehart & Winston, 1984.

Kirkup, James, trans,. Three poems, in A. R. Davis, ed., *Modern
Japanese Poetry.* St. Lucia: University of Queensland
Press, 1978.

Miyamori, Asatarō, trans. Thirteen poems, in his *Masterpieces of
Japanese Poetry, Ancient and Modern.* Tokyo: Maruzen,
1936.

Rexroth, Kenneth, trans. Three poems, in his *In Defense of the
Earth.* New York: New Directions, 1956.

Sakanishi, Shio, trans. *A Handful of Sand.* Boston: Marshall
Jones, 1934.

Sesar, Carl, trans. *Poems to Eat.* Tokyo: Kodansha International,
1966.

Satō, Hiroaki, trans. Forty-seven poems, in Hiroaki Satō, and Bur-
ton Watson, eds., *From the Country of Eight Islands.* Gar-
den City, N.Y.: Anchor Press, 1981.

Takamine, Hiroshi, trans. *A Sad Toy.* Tokyo: Tokyo News Ser-
vice, 1962.

Viglielmo, V. H., trans. Seven poems, in Yoshie Okazaki, *Japa-
nese Literature in the Meiji Era.* Tokyo: Obunsha, 1955.

Yasuda, Shōson, trans. Three poems, in his *Lacquer Box.* Tokyo:
Nippon Times, 1952.

Other Writings in Translation
"Rōmaji Diary," trans. by Donald Keene. In his *Modern Japa-
nese Literature.* New York: Grove Press, 1956.

Biographical and Critical Studies
Hijiya, Yukihiko. *Ishikawa Takuboku.* Boston: Twayne, 1979.

Keene, Donald. "Shiki and Takuboku." In his *Landscapes and
Portraits.* Tokyo: Kodansha International, 1971.

———. "The Diaries of Ishikawa Takuboku." In his *Modern Jap-
anese Diaries.* New York: Henry Holt, 1995.

Ueda, Makoto. "Ishikawa Takuboku." In his *Modern Japanese Po-
ets and the Nature of Literature.* Stanford: Stanford Univer-
sity Press, 1983.

KITAHARA HAKUSHŪ
Tanka in Translation
Honda, H. H., trans. One poem, in his *From Spring to Winter.*
Tokyo: Hokuseido, 1960.

Keene, Donald, trans. Eight poems, in his *Dawn to the West.*
New York: Holt, Rinehart & Winston, 1984.

Miyamori, Asatarō, trans. Seven poems, in his *Masterpieces of*

Japanese Poetry, Ancient and Modern. Tokyo: Maruzen, 1936.

Viglielmo, V. H., trans. Seven poems, in Yoshie Okazaki, *Japanese Literature in the Meiji Era.* Tokyo: Obunsha, 1955.

Shionozaki, Hiroshi, trans. Two poems, in *The Tanka Journal,* no. 2 (1993).

Yasuda, Shōson, trans. Three poems, in his *Lacquer Box.* Tokyo: Nippon Times, 1952.

Biographical and Critical Studies

Fukasawa, Margaret Benton. "Kitahara Hakushū: His Life and Poetry." Ph.D. diss., Columbia University, 1977.

Satō, Hiroaki. "Kitahara Hakushū." In *Kodansha Encyclopedia of Japan.* Tokyo: Kodansha International, 1983.

KONDŌ YOSHIMI

Tanka in Translation

Huey, Robert N., trans. One poem, in Japan P.E.N. Club, *A Survey of Japanese Literature Today.* Tokyo: Japan P.E.N. Club, 1984.

Keene, Donald, trans. Two poems, in his *Dawn to the West.* New York: Holt, Rinehart & Winston, 1984.

Noritoshi, Susumu. Five poems, in *The Tanka Journal,* no. 2 (1993).

MAEKAWA SAMIO

Tanka in Translation

Huey, Robert N., trans. One poem, in Japan P.E.N. Club, *A Survey of Japanese Literature Today.* Tokyo: Japan P.E.N. Club, 1984.

MASAOKA SHIKI

Tanka in Translation

Asatarō, Miyamori, trans. Three poems, in his *Masterpieces of Japanese Poetry, Ancient and Modern.* Tokyo: Maruzen, 1936.

Bownas, Geoffrey and Anthony Thwaite, trans. Two poems, in their *The Penguin Book of Japanese Verse.* Baltimore: Penguin Books, 1964.

Carter, Steven D., trans. Eight poems, in his *Traditional Japanese Poetry.* Stanford: Stanford University Press, 1991.

Keene, Donald, trans. Three poems, in his *Dawn to the West.* New York: Holt, Rinehart & Winston, 1984.

Honda, H. H., trans. Nine poems, in *The Reeds,* no. 3 (1957).

———. Forty-two poems, ibid., no. 4 (1958).

Shōson, Yasuda, trans. Three poems, in his *Lacquer Box*. Tokyo: Nippon Times, 1952.

Viglielmo, V. H., trans. Nine poems, in Yoshie Okazaki, *Japanese Literature in the Meiji Era*. Tokyo: Obunsha, 1955.

Watson, Burton, trans. Fifteen poems, in Hiroaki Satō and Burton Watson, eds., *From the Country of Eight Islands*. Garden City, N.Y.: Anchor Press, 1981.

Other Writings in Translation

"My Six-Foot World," trans. by Laura R. Rodd. In *Voices* 3, no.1 (1975).

"The Verse Record of My Peonies," trans. by Earl Miner. In his *Japanese Poetic Diaries*. Berkeley: University of California Press, 1969.

Biographical and Critical Studies

Beichman, Janine. *Masaoka Shiki*. Boston: Twayne, 1982.

Beichman-Yamamoto, Janine. "Masaoka Shiki's 'A Drop of Ink.' " In *Monumenta Nipponica* 30, no. 3 (1975).

Brower, Robert H. "Masaoka Shiki and Tanka Reform." In Donald H. Shively, ed., *Tradition and Modernization in Japanese Culture*. Princeton: Princeton University Press, 1971.

Keene, Donald. "Shiki and Takuboku." In his *Landscapes and Portraits*. Tokyo: Kodansha International, 1971.

———."Masaoka Shiki." In his *Some Japanese Portraits*. Tokyo: Kodansha International, 1978.

———. "The Diaries of Masaoka Shiki." In his *Modern Japanese Diaries*. New York: Henry Holt, 1995.

Ueda, Makoto. "Masaoka Shiki." In his *Modern Japanese Poets and the Nature of Literature*. Stanford: Stanford University Press, 1983.

MIYA SHŪJI

Tanka in Translation

Huey, Robert N., trans. One poem, in Japan P.E.N. Club, *A Survey of Japanese Literature Today*. Tokyo: Japan P.E.N. Club, 1984.

Keene, Donald, trans. One poem, in his *Landscapes and Portraits*. Tokyo: Kodansha International, 1971.

Okuda, Machiko, trans. Five poems, in *The Tanka Journal*, no. 6 (1995).

Takehisa, Akiko, trans. Six poems, in *The Tanka Journal*, no. 4 (1994).

———. Six poems, ibid., no. 5 (1995).

MIYAZAWA KENJI
Free Verse in Translation
Ninomiya, Takamichi and D. J. Enright, trans. Four poems, in
    their *The Poetry of Living Japan*. London: John Murray,
    1957.
Satō, Hiroaki, trans. *Spring and Asura*, Chicago: Chicago Review
    Press, 1973.
Snyder, Gary, trans. Eighteen poems, in his *The Back Country*.
    New York: New Directions, 1957.

Prose Fiction in Translation
Night of the Milky Way Railway, trans. by Sarah M. Strong. Ar-
    monk, N.Y.: Sharpe, 1991.
Wildcats and the Acorns, trans. by John Bester. Tokyo: Kodansha
    International, 1985.
Winds and Wildcat Places: Stories by Miyazawa Kenji, trans. by
    John Bester. Tokyo: Kodansha International, 1967.
Winds from Afar, trans. by John Bester. Tokyo: Kodansha Interna-
    tional, 1972.

Biographical and Critical Studies
Fromm, Mallory. "The Ideals of Miyazawa Kenji: A Critical Ac-
    count of Their Genesis, Development and Literary Expres-
    sions." Ph.D. diss., University of London, 1980.
Hagiwara, Takao. "The Theme of Innocence in Miyazawa Kenji's
    Tales." Ph.D. diss., University of British Columbia, 1986.
———. "Innocence and the Other World: The Tales of Miya-
    zawa Kenji." In *Monumenta Nipponica* 47, no. 2 (1992).
Nakajima, Kenzō. "Miyazawa Kenji, the Man and His Works."
    In *Japan Quarterly* 5, no. 1 (1958).
Strong, Sarah M. "The Poetry of Miyazawa Kenji." Ph.D. diss.,
    University of Chicago, 1984.
———. "Miyazawa Kenji and the Lost Gandharan Painting." In
    Monumenta Nipponica 41, no. 2 (1986).
Ueda, Makoto. "Miyazawa Kenji." In his *Modern Japanese Poets
    and the Nature of Literature*. Stanford: Stanford University
    Press, 1983.

MORI ŌGAI
Tanka in Translation
Miyamori Asatarō, trans. One poem, in his *Masterpieces of Japa-
    nese Poetry, Ancient and Modern*. Tokyo: Maruzen, 1936.

Prose Fiction in Translation
The Historical Fiction of Mori Ōgai, trans. by David Dilworth et
    al. Honolulu: University of Hawaii Press, 1991.

Vita Sexualis, trans. by Kazuji Ninomiya and Sanford Goldstein. Rutland, Vt.: Tuttle, 1972.

The Wild Geese, trans. by Kingo Ochiai and Sanford Goldstein. Rutland, Vt.: Tuttle, 1959.

Youth and Other Stories, trans. by J. Thomas Rimer et al. Honolulu: University of Hawaii Press, 1994.

Biographical and Critical Studies

Bowring, Richard John. *Mori Ōgai and the Modernization of Japanese Culture.* Cambridge: Cambridge University Press, 1979.

Hasegawa, Izumi. "Mori Ōgai." *Japan Quarterly* 12, no. 2 (1965).

Hopper, Helen Marlys. "The Conflict between Japanese Tradition and Western Learning in the Meiji Intellectual Mori Ōgai." Ph.D. diss., Washington University, 1976.

Johnson, Eric W. "Mori Ōgai: The Fiction from 1909 to Early 1914." Ph.D. diss., University of Chicago, 1973.

Lewell, John. "Mori Ōgai." In his *Modern Japanese Novelists.* Tokyo: Kodansha International, 1993.

Marcus, Marvin. *Paragons of the Ordinary: The Biographical Literature of Mori Ōgai.* Honolulu: University of Hawaii Press, 1993.

Nakai, Yoshiyuki. "The Young Mori Ōgai, 1862–1892." Ph.D. diss., Harvard University, 1974.

Rimer, J. Thomas. *Mori Ōgai.* Boston: Twayne, 1975.

NAKAJŌ FUMIKO
Tanka in Translation

Huey, Robert N. trans. One poem, in Japan P.E.N. Club, *A Survey of Japanese Literature Today.* Tokyo: Japan P.E.N. Club, 1984.

OKAMOTO KANOKO
Tanka in Translation

Lewis, Richard, trans. One poem, in his *The Moment of Wonder.* New York: Dial Press, 1964.

Miyamori, Asatarō, trans. Three tanka, in his *Masterpieces of Japanese Literature, Ancient and Modern.* Tokyo: Maruzen, 1936.

Rexroth, Kenneth and Ikuko Atsumi, trans. One poem, in their *The Burning Heart.* New York: Seabury Press, 1977.

Yasuda, Shōson, trans. One poem, in his *Lacquer Box.* Tokyo: Nippon Times, 1952.

Prose Fiction in Translation
"A Floral Pageant," trans. by Hiroko Morita Malatesta. In Yukiko
  Tanaka, ed., *To Live and To Write*. Seattle: Seal Press,
  1987.
"A Mother's Love," trans. by Phyllis Birnbaum. In her *Rabbits,
  Crabs, Etc.: Stories by Japanese Women*. Honolulu: Univer-
  sity of Hawaii Press, 1982.
"Scarlet Flower," trans. by Edward Seidensticker. In *Japan Quar-
  terly* 10, no. 3 (1963).
The Tale of an Old Geisha and Other Stories, trans. by Kazuko
  Sugisaki. Santa Barbara, Calif.: Capra Press, 1985.

Biographical and Critical Studies
Lewell, John. "Okamoto Kanoko." In his *Modern Japanese Novel-
  ists*. Tokyo: Kodansha International, 1993.
Mori, Maryellen Toman. "The Quest Motif in the Fiction of
  Okamoto Kanoko." Ph.D. diss., Harvard University, 1988.
Sugisaki, Kazuko. "Harmonious Motion of Life: A Comparative
  Study of the Works of Katherine Anne Porter and Kanoko
  Okamoto." Ph.D. diss., Occidental College, 1973.

TAWARA MACHI
Tanka in Translation
Carpenter, Juliet Winters, trans. *Salad Anniversary*. Tokyo: Ko-
  dansha International, 1989.
Carpenter, Juliet Winters, trans. Four poems, in *Japanese Litera-
  ture Today*, no. 17 (1992).
Lowitz, Leza, Miyuki Aoyama, and Akemi Tomioka, trans. Nine
  poems, in their *A Long Rainy Season*. Berkeley, Calif.:
  Stone Bridge Press, 1994.
Stamm, Jack, trans. *Salad Anniversary*. Tokyo: Kawade Shobō
  Shinsha, 1988.

TOKI ZENMARO (AIKA)
Tanka in Translation
Keene, Donald, trans. Five poems, in his *Dawn to the West*.
  New York: Holt, Rinehart & Winston, 1984.
Miyamori, Asatarō, trans. Four poems, in his *Masterpieces of Po-
  etry, Ancient and Modern*. Tokyo: Maruzen, 1936.
Putzar, Edward, trans. One poem, in his *Japanese Literature*.
  Tucson: University of Arizona Press, 1973.
Viglielmo, V. H., trans. Three poems, in Yoshie Okazaki, *Japa-
  nese Literature in the Meiji Era*. Tokyo: Obunsha, 1955.

Yasuda, Shōson, trans. One poem, in his *Lacquer Box*. Tokyo: Nippon Times, 1952.

Biographical and Critical Studies
Hisamatsu, Sen'ichi. "Toki Zenmaro." In his *Biographical Dictionary of Japanese Literature*. Tokyo: Kodansha International, 1976.

TSUKAMOTO KUNIO
Tanka in Translation
Bownas, Geoffrey, trans. Five poems, in Yukio Mishima and Geoffrey Bownas, eds., *New Writing in Japan*. Baltimore: Penguin Books, 1972.
Huey, Robert N., trans. One poem, in Japan P.E.N. Club, *A Survey of Japanese Literature Today*. Tokyo: Japan P.E.N. Club, 1984.
Keene, Donald, trans. Three poems, in his *Dawn to the West*. New York: Holt, Rinehart & Winston, 1984.
Kobayashi, Takao, trans. Five poems, in *The Tanka Journal*, no. 6 (1995).
Nakagawa, Atsuo, trans. Five poems, in *The Tanka Journal*, no. 2 (1993).
Nakagawa, Onsey, trans. Two poems, in *Poetry Nippon 88* (1989).

SAITŌ FUMI
Tanka in Translation
Honda, H. H., trans. One poem, in his *From Spring to Winter*. Tokyo: Hokuseido, 1960.
Huey, Robert N., trans. One poem, in Japan P.E.N. Club, *A Survey of Japanese Literature Today*. Tokyo: Japan P.E.N. Club, 1984.
Lowitz, Leza, Miyuki Aoyama, and Akemi Tomioka, trans. Eleven poems, in their *A Long Rainy Season*. Berkeley, Calif.: Stone Bridge Press, 1994.
Shiffert, Edith Marcombe and Yūki Sawa, trans. Twelve poems, in their *Anthology of Modern Japanese Poetry*. Rutland, Vt.: Tuttle, 1972.
Yasuda, Shōson, trans. One poem, in his *Lacquer Box*. Tokyo: Nippon Times, 1952.

SAITŌ MOKICHI
Tanka in Translation
Bownas, Geoffrey and Anthony Thwaite, trans. Five poems, in their *The Penguin Book of Japanese Verse*. Baltimore: Penguin Books, 1964.

Carter, Steven D., trans. Four poems, in his *Traditional Japanese Poetry*. Stanford: Stanford University Press, 1991.

Hibbett, Howard, trans. Four poems, in Donald Keene, ed., *Modern Japanese Literature*. New York: Grove Press, 1956.

Keene, Donald, trans. Nine poems, in his *Dawn to the West*. New York: Holt, Rinehart & Winston, 1984.

Miyamori, Asatarō, trans. Eight poems, in his *Masterpieces of Japanese Poetry, Ancient and Modern*. Tokyo: Maruzen, 1936.

Satō, Hiroaki, trans. Fifty-nine poems, in Hiroaki Satō and Burton Watson, eds., *From the Country of Eight Islands*. Garden City, N.Y.: Anchor Press, 1981.

Shiffert, Edith Marcombe and Yūki Sawa, trans. Thirteen poems, in their *Anthology of Modern Japanese Poetry*. Rutland, Vt.: Tuttle, 1972.

Shinoda, Seishi and Sanford Goldstein, trans. *Red Lights*. West Lafayette, Ind.: Purdue University Press, 1989.

Viglielmo, V. H., trans. Five poems, in Yoshie Okazaki, *Japanese Literature in the Meiji Era*. Tokyo: Obunsha, 1955.

Yasuda, Shōson, trans. Four poems, in his *Lacquer Box*. Tokyo: Nippon Times, 1952.

Biographical and Critical Studies

Heinrich, Amy Vladeck. " 'My Mother is Dying': Saitō Mokichi's 'Shinitamau Haha.' " In *Monumenta Nipponica* 33, no. 4 (1978).

———. *Fragments of Rainbows: The Life and Poetry of Saitō Mokichi*. New York: Columbia University Press, 1983.

Hisamatsu, Sen'ichi. "Saitō Mokichi." In his *Biographical Dictionary of Japanese Literature*. Tokyo: Kodansha International, 1976.

SHAKU CHŌKŪ (ORIKUCHI SHINOBU)

Tanka in Translation

Keene, Donald, trans. Seven poems, in his *Dawn to the West*. New York: Holt, Rinehart & Winston, 1984.

Philippi, Donald, trans. Twenty-two poems, in *Today's Japan* 11, no. 1 (1961).

Yasuda, Shōson, trans. Two poems, in his *Lacquer Box*. Tokyo: Nippon Times, 1952.

Other Writings in Translation

"A Study of Life in Ancient Days." In *Traditions* 1, no. 4 (1977).

Biographical and Critical Studies

Harootunian, H. D. "Disciplinizing Native Knowledge and Producing Place: Yanagita Kunio, Origuchi Shinobu, Takata

Yasuma." In J. Thomas Rimer, ed., *Culture and Identity.*
Princeton: Princeton University Press, 1990.

Hinotani, Akihiko. "Orikuchi Shinobu." In *Kodansha Encyclopedia of Japan.* Tokyo: Kodansha International, 1983.

Hisamatsu, Sen'ichi. "Origuchi Shinobu." In his *Biographical Dictionary of Japanese Literature.* Tokyo: Kodansha International, 1976.

YOSANO AKIKO
Tanka in Translation

Atsumi, Ikuko and Graeme Wilson, trans. Ten poems, in *Japan Quarterly* 21, no. 2 (1974).

Bownas, Geoffrey and Anthony Thwaite, trans. Four poems, in their *The Penguin Book of Japanese Verse.* Baltimore: Penguin Books, 1964.

Carter, Steven D., trans. Seven poems, in his *Traditional Japanese Poetry.* Stanford: Stanford University Press, 1991.

Cranston, Edwin A., trans. Ninety-eight poems, in *Journal of the Association of Teachers of Japanese* 25, no. 1 (1991).

Eleven poems (anonymous translator). In Kokusai Bunka Shinkōkai, ed., *Introduction to Classic Japanese Literature.* Tokyo: Kokusai Bunka Shinkōkai, 1948.

Goldstein, Sanford and Seishi Shinoda, trans. *Tangled Hair.* Lafayette, Ind.: Purdue University Studies, 1971.

Hisamatsu, Sen'ichi, trans. Three poems in *Biographical Dictionary of Japanese Literature.* Tokyo: Kodansha International, 1976.

Honda, H. H., trans. *The Poetry of Yosano Akiko.* Tokyo: Hokuseido, 1957.

Hughes, Glenn and Yozan T. Iwasaki, trans. Thirty poems, in their *Three Women Poets of Modern Japan.* Seattle: University of Washington Book Store, 1927.

Keene, Donald, trans. Three poems, in his *Dawn to the West.* New York: Holt, Rinehart & Winston, 1984.

Maloney, Dennis and Hide Oshiro, trans. *Tangled Hair.* Fredonia, N.Y.: White Pine Press, 1987.

Miyamori, Asatarō, trans. Sixteen poems, in his *Masterpieces of Japanese Poetry, Ancient and Modern.* Tokyo: Maruzen, 1936.

O'Brien, James, trans. Nineteen poems, in *Journal of the Association of Teachers of Japanese* 25, no. 1 (1991).

Rexroth, Kenneth and Ikuko Atsumi, trans. Eleven poems, in their *The Burning Heart.* New York: Seabury Press, 1977.

Sakanishi, Shio, trans. *Tangled Hair.* Boston: Marshall Jones, 1935.

Satō, Hiroaki, trans. Thirty-nine poems, in Hiroaki Satō and Burton Watson, eds., *From the Country of Eight Islands.* Garden City, N.Y.: Anchor Press, 1981.

Viglielmo, V. H., trans. Eleven poems, in Yoshie Okazaki, *Japanese Literature in the Meiji Era.* Tokyo: Obunsha, 1955.

Yasuda, Shōson, trans. Three poems, in his *Lacquer Box.* Tokyo: Nippon Times, 1952.

Biographical and Critical Studies

Beichman, Janine. "Yosano Akiko: The Early Years." In *Japan Quarterly* 37, no. 1 (1990).

———. "Yosano Akiko: Return to the Female." In ibid. 37, no. 2 (1990).

Cranston, Edwin A. "Young Akiko: The Literary Debut of Yosano Akiko." In *Literature East and West* 28, no. 1 (1974).

Larson, Phyllis Hyland. "Yosano Akiko: The Early Years." Ph.D. diss., University of Minnesota, 1985.

Rodd, Laurel Rasplica. "Yosano Akiko and the Taishō Debate over the 'New Woman.' " In Gail Lee Bernstein, ed., *Recreating Japanese Women.* Berkeley: University of California Press, 1991.

———. guest ed. Special issue on Yosano Akiko. *Journal of the Association of Teachers of Japanese* 25, no. 1 (1991).

Ueda, Makoto. "Yosano Akiko." In his *Modern Japanese Poets and the Nature of Literature.* Stanford: Stanford University Press, 1983.

YOSANO TEKKAN (HIROSHI)

Tanka in Translation

Brower, Robert H., trans. Two poems, in Donald H. Shively, ed., *Tradition and Modernization in Japanese Culture.* Princeton: Princeton University Press, 1971.

Honda, H. H., trans. One poem, in his *From Spring to Winter.* Tokyo: Hokuseido, 1960.

Keene, Donald, trans. Eight poems, in his *Dawn to the West.* New York: Holt, Rinehart & Winston, 1984.

Miyamori, Asatarō, trans. Fourteen poems, in his *Masterpieces of Japanese Poetry, Ancient and Modern.* Tokyo: Maruzen, 1936.

Two poems (anonymous translator). In Kokusai Bunka Shinkō-kai, ed., *Introduction to Classic Japanese Literature.* Tokyo: Kokusai Bunka Shinkōkai, 1948.

Viglielmo, V. H., trans. Seven poems, in Yoshie Okazaki, *Japanese Literature in the Meiji Era.* Tokyo: Obunsha, 1955.

Yasuda, Shōson, trans. Two poems, in his *Lacquer Box*. Tokyo: Nippon Times, 1952.

Biographical and Critical Studies
Hisamatsu, Sen'ichi. "Yosano Hiroshi." In his *Biographical Dictionary of Japanese Literature*. Tokyo: Kodansha International, 1976.

Copyright
Acknowledgments

The compiler thanks the following poets and their heirs for permission to translate and publish these poems:

Yosano Tekkan: "no ni ouru" from *Tōzai nanboku* (1896); "shide no yama" from *Tekkanshi* (1901); "nasake sugite" from *Murasaki* (1901); "Afurika no" from *Dokugusa* (1904); "nai no asa," "waga uchi ni," "ibo arite," "sono chichi wa," "keshi sakinu," "hebi kitsune," and "niwatori no" from *Sōmon* (1910); "hiza no ue ni," "usujiroku," "ugokazaru," and "tsubutsubu to" from *Karasu to ame* (1915); "mizukara no," "afururu wa," "naki ni naku," "chichi ni ninu," and "oto mo naku" from *Yosano Hiroshi tanka zenshū* (1933).

Masaoka Shiki: all selections from Kawahigashi Hekigodō et al., eds., Shiki zenshū (Kaizōsha, 1929–1931).

Mori Ōgai: "uta mo kakare" and "aozora no" from *Uta nikki* (1907); "chiriboeru," "ochi kochi ni," "hi wo torite," "satogawa no kishibe," "fujinami no," "samidare no," "fumoto ni wa," and "satogawa no nagare" from *Tokiwakai eisō 1* (1909); "shimeritaru" from *Myōjō*, Oct. 1907; "nami wo kiru" from *Myōjō*, Jan. 1908; "hi hitohi" from *Myōjō*, Aug. 1908; "kainadeba," "mikokoro wa," "kunshō wa," "nani hitotsu," and "kuruoshiki" from *Subaru*, May 1909; "Narabito wa" and "ōgane wo" from *Myōjō*, Jan. 1922.

Yosano Akiko: "noroiuta," "hoshi to narite," "mune no shimizu," "chibusa osae," "harusamu no," "tsubaki sore," "wakaki oyubi," and "uta no te ni" from *Midaregami* (1901); "konjiki no" from *Koigoromo* (1905); "tatakai wa," "kazashitaru," and "hanshin ni" from *Maihime* (1906); "chi wa hitotsu" and "hisakata no" from *Yume no hana* (1906); "mune no umi" from *Tokonatsu* (1908); "ii shiranu" from *Saohime* (1909); "akuryō to" from *Seikaiha* (1912); "shion saku" from

Taiyō to bara (1921); "kokoro naru" and "ko no ma naru" from *Hakuōshū* (1942).

Ishikawa Takuboku: "tawamure ni," "waga naku wo," "akiretaru," "kagami tori," "michibata ni," "kemono meku," "hatarakedo," "nani ga nashi ni," "shiroki hasu," and "mizu no goto" from *Ichiaku no suna* (1910); "iki sureba," "me tozuredo," "ayamachite," "bon'yari to," "omou koto," "atarashiki, "unmei no," "kanashiku mo," "yaya tōki," and "aruhi, futo" from *Kanashiki gangu* (1912).

Saitō Mokichi and Saitō Yuka: "akanasu no," "niwatori no," "ichimen ni," "Googan no," "yo no iro no," "ama kirashi," "mendorira," "sube naki ka," and "daariya wa" from *Shakkō* (1913); "hitaburu ni" and "dentō no" from *Aratama* (1921); "inochi shinishi" from *Henreki* (1948); "maotome no" from *Kan'un* (1940); "anmaku wo" from *Shōen* (1949); "kano kishi ni," "atarashiki," "michi no be ni," and "ana ideshi" from *Shiroki yama* (1949); "waga ikishi" and "ametsuchi no" from *Tsukikage* (1954).

Kitahara Hakushū: "haru no tori," "shiore yuku," "tasogare no," "kyō mo mata," "sutaretaru," "yameru ko wa," "yubisaki no," "inakaya ni," "futonegi no," "hirugedoki," and "natsu wa sabishi" from *Kiri no hana* (1913); "mika no tsuki" from *Kirarashū* (1915); "hiru nagara" and "mazushisa ni" from *Suzume no tamago* (1921); "hoo no hana" from *Shira hae* (1934); "kichikō wa" from *Tsurubami* (1943); "yuku mizu no" from *Keiryū shō* (1943); "fuyu hiyaki" and "gasorin" from *Kurohi* (1940); "hito sekite" from *Botan no boku* (1943).

Shaku Chōkū and Orikuchi Yasumi: "dono ko no," "joya no kane," "nagaki hi no," "kisha hashiru," "keshiki tatsu," "minasoko ni," "nemu no ha no," and "kuzu no hana" from *Umi yama no aida* (1925); "kuriyabe no," "yo no naka ni," and "machi no ko no" from *Haru no kotobure* (1930); "isamashiki," "mihotoke no," and "muragarite" from *Tōyamahiko* (1948); "tōtsu yo no," "hitokadoi," "ōkinaru," "kimyōnaru," "ikuhyaku no," and "yaso tanjōe" from *Yamato oguna* (1955).

Toki Zenmaro and Toki Kenji: "te no shiroki," "Nippon ni," and "hatarakanu" from *Tasogare ni* (1912); "namida, namida" from *Fuhei naku* (1913); "muttsuri to," "waga shirenu,"

Sasaki Yukitsuna: "hashiranai," "futorigimi no," "kagaku kigō," and "ware no yakishi" from *Gunrei* (1970); "gekkō ni," "futsukayoi no," "shinkōkei wo," "tomarazaru," and "henseiki" from *Chokuritsu seyo ichigyō no shi* (1972); "shiika to wa" and "semi no kago wo" from *Natsu no kagami* (1976); "chiri oeshi," "tomo no shi ni," "kamisori no," "soranjite," "tabisaki ni," "owaruru yume," "izure ka ichiwa," "genshoku no," and "ko wo daite" from *Hanka* (1989).

Tawara Machi: "ochite kita," "ichi purasu," "30 made," "haru wo matsu," "tegami ni wa," "kakioete," "mishi koto no," "sakura sakura," and "tenki yohō" from *Sarada kinenbi* (1987); "shibaraku wa," "shakai to no," "kimi no ko wo," "zō to iu," "nibun no ichibyō," "itsumo yori," "iroenpitsu no," "uminari ni," "umioeshi," "mienu kara," and "furusato no" from *Kaze no tenohira* (1991).

Other
Works
in the
Columbia
Asian
Studies
Series

Modern Asian Literature Series

Translations from the Asian Classics

Major Plays of Chikamatsu, tr. Donald Keene   1961

Four Major Plays of Chikamatsu, tr. Donald Keene. Paper-
  back ed. only.   1961

*Records of the Grand Historian of China, translated from the
  Shih chi of Ssu-ma Ch'ien,* tr. Burton Watson, 2 vols.   1961

*Instructions for Practical Living and Other Neo-Confucian
  Writings by Wang Yang-ming,* tr. Wing-tsit Chan   1963

Chuang Tzu: Basic Writings, tr. Burton Watson, paperback
  ed. only.   1964

The Mahābhārata, tr. Chakravarthi V. Narasimhan. Also in
  paperback ed.   1965

The Manyōshū, Nippon Gakujutsu Shinkōkai edition   1965

Su Tung-p'o: Selections from a Sung Dynasty Poet, tr. Burton
  Watson. Also in paperback ed.   1965

Bhartrihari: Poems, tr. Barbara Stoler Miller. Also in paper-
  back ed.   1967

Basic Writings of Mo Tzu, Hsün Tzu, and Han Fei Tzu, tr.
  Burton Watson. Also in separate paperback eds.   1967

The Awakening of Faith, Attributed to Aśvaghosha, tr.
  Yoshito S. Hakeda. Also in paperback ed.   1967

*Reflections on Things at Hand: The Neo-Confucian Anthol-
  ogy,* comp. Chu Hsi and Lü Tsu-ch'ien, tr. Wing-tsit
  Chan   1967

The Platform Sutra of the Sixth Patriarch, tr. Philip B. Yam-
  polsky. Also in paperback ed.   1967

Essays in Idleness: The Tsurezuregusa of Kenkō, tr. Donald
  Keene. Also in paperback ed.   1967

The Pillow Book of Sei Shōnagon, tr. Ivan Morris, 2 vols.   1967

*Two Plays of Ancient India: The Little Clay Cart and the
  Minister's Seal,* tr. J. A. B. van Buitenen   1968

The Complete Works of Chuang Tzu, tr. Burton Watson   1968

The Romance of the Western Chamber (Hsi Hsiang chi), tr.
  S. I. Hsiung. Also in paperback ed.   1968

The Manyōshū, Nippon Gakujutsu Shinkōkai edition. Paper-
  back ed. only.   1969

*Records of the Historian: Chapters from the Shih chi of Ssu-
  ma Ch'ien,* tr. Burton Watson. Paperback ed. only.   1969

Cold Mountain: 100 Poems by the T'ang Poet Han-shan, tr.
  Burton Watson. Also in paperback ed.   1970

Twenty Plays of the Nō Theatre, ed. Donald Keene. Also in
  paperback ed.   1970

Chūshingura: The Treasury of Loyal Retainers, tr. Donald
  Keene. Also in paperback ed.   1971

The Zen Master Hakuin: Selected Writings, tr. Philip B. Yam-
  polsky   1971

The Bhagavad Gita: Krishna's Counsel in Time of War, tr. Barbara Stoler Miller — 1986

The Columbia Book of Later Chinese Poetry, ed. and tr. Jonathan Chaves. Also in paperback ed. — 1986

The Tso Chuan: Selections from China's Oldest Narrative History, tr. Burton Watson — 1989

Waiting for the Wind: Thirty-six Poets of Japan's Late Medieval Age, tr. Steven Carter — 1989

Selected Writings of Nichiren, ed. Philip B. Yampolsky — 1990

Saigyō, Poems of a Mountain Home, tr. Burton Watson — 1990

The Book of Lieh-Tzu: A Classic of the Tao, tr. A. C. Graham. Morningside ed. — 1990

The Tale of an Anklet: An Epic of South India: The Cilappatikāram of Iḷaṅkō Aṭikaḷ, tr. R. Parthasarathy — 1993

Waiting for the Dawn: A Plan for the Prince, tr. and introduction by Wm. Theodore de Bary — 1993

The Lotus Sutra, tr. Burton Watson. Also in paperback ed. — 1993

The Classic of Changes: A New Translation of the I Ching as Interpreted by Wang Bi, tr. Richard John Lynn — 1994

Beyond Spring: Poems of the Sung Dynasty, tr. Julie Landau — 1994

The Columbia Anthology of Traditional Chinese Literature, ed. Victor H. Mair — 1994

Scenes for Mandarins: The Elite Theater of the Ming, tr. Cyril Birch — 1995

Studies in Asian Culture

1. *The Ōnin War: History of Its Origins and Background, with a Selective Translation of the Chronicle of Ōnin*, by H. Paul Varley — 1967

2. *Chinese Government in Ming Times: Seven Studies*, ed. Charles O. Hucker — 1969

3. *The Actors' Analects (Yakusha Rongo)*, ed. and tr. by Charles J. Dunn and Bunzō Torigoe — 1969

4. *Self and Society in Ming Thought*, by Wm. Theodore de Bary and the Conference on Ming Thought. Also in paperback ed. — 1970

5. *A History of Islamic Philosophy*, by Majid Fakhry, 2d ed. — 1983

6. *Phantasies of a Love Thief: The Caurapañcāśikā Attributed to Bilhaṇa*, by Barbara Stoler Miller — 1971

7. *Iqbal: Poet-Philosopher of Pakistan*, ed. Hafeez Malik — 1971

8. *The Golden Tradition: An Anthology of Urdu Poetry*, ed. and tr. Ahmed Ali. Also in paperback ed. — 1973

9. *Conquerors and Confucians: Aspects of Political Change in Late Yüan China*, by John W. Dardess — 1973

10. *The Unfolding of Neo-Confucianism*, by Wm. Theodore de Bary and the Conference on Seventeenth-Century Chinese Thought. Also in paperback ed. — 1975

Companions to Asian Studies

Introduction to Asian Civilizations
Wm. Theodore de Bary, Editor

Neo-Confucian Studies

.

Designer: Teresa Bonner
Text: Electra
Compositor: Maple Vail
Printer: Maple Vail
Binder: Maple Vail